A Life in Writing

Michael Byrne

A Life in Writing

for my family

A Life in Writing
ISBN 978 1 76041 978 3
Copyright © text Michael Byrne 2020
Cover photo: reading poetry to Avery at Tuross

First published 2020 by
GINNINDERRA PRESS
PO Box 3461 Port Adelaide 5015
www.ginninderrapress.com.au

Contents

Foreword	7
Early Childhood	9
Kindergarten to Year 2	11
Years 3 to 6	13
Years 7 and 8	16
Year 9	20
Year 10	23
Year 11	25
Year 12	29
1997	34
1998	38
1999	42
2000	46
2001	51
2002	55
2003	62
2004	66
2005	71
2006	74
2007	79
2008	85
2009	88
2010	91
2011	94
2012	97
2013	100

2014	104
2015	106
2016	109
2017–April 2018	114
My Poetry	118
Regular Reading Gigs	120
My Books	122
Epilogue	125
Articles and Reviews	127

Foreword

This autobiography charts the evolution of Michael Byrne as an award-winning poet in the Australian Capital Territory. It explores, through vignettes his early life, the awakening of his desire to become a poet, his time as the new kid on the block and his arrival as a mature poet. Along the way, examples of his developing poetry are shared with the reader. The process in learning his craft, familiar to all poets, is set out with its associated highs and lows.

At the same time, the autobiography also chronicles the decline in Michael's mental health from his teenage years to the present time. It explores the link between his serious mental health issues and his poetry writing. It gives some insight into the difficulties his mental health has presented in achieving his dreams in some areas of his life.

However, in spite of these difficulties, Michael has had four collections of poetry published. He has also edited two published anthologies. A number of these books have been award-winners. Michael's poetry has been included in numerous poetry anthologies, including an anthology of the best of Australian poetry. His poetry has been performed on stage. In addition, he has been able to complete two university degrees and become a much-loved uncle.

Michael Byrne's frank, raw but often funny account of his first forty years paints a picture of an intelligent, creative, determined, sensitive and humorous man. He also happens to be the best son a father could have.

Phil Byrne

Early Childhood

The first memory I have is of when I was two, possibly three. I was riding my tricycle in the driveway of my house. It's a pleasant memory – everything was as simple as that.

*

Apparently, my mum withdrew me from crèche because I was getting picked on. I can't remember that happening. From what I can remember, preschool was okay.

*

I can't remember this but apparently Richard's mum and my mum were talking at our place while Richard (a boy in my year at school) and I were looking at each other. Then Richard pushed me over and I cried. Boys, even at that age, can be rough. Years later, I witnessed the same thing happen to a boy at the Florey shops, near where I lived. I felt so sorry for him that I gave him some of my biscuit that I had bought from the bakery and he stopped crying. His parents liked it and it made me feel good inside.

*

At preschool, one of the teachers sang me a song: 'You've got the whole world in your hands, you've got the whole world in your hands, you've got the whole world in your hands, you've got the whole world in your hands'. Even at that age, I had an emotional reaction to it, like it really meant something to me.

*

I remember having a girlfriend when I was three but as we went into a supermarket she told me she was no longer my girlfriend. I can't remember her name. It stung a bit, not as much as an adult relationship break-up. But it still hurt.

*

I used to wrap myself up in curtains. I liked creating my own little world. Also, I used to create my own little world with bedsheets and pretend I was on the moon.

*

I was basically a happy kid at this age. My parents were together and good parents. I was optimistic about the future. Whatever school was, I was confident I could handle it.

Kindergarten to Year 2

The first day of school: I was about to cry then I spotted Luke (my best mate). He was going to be in my class. Things were looking up.

*

In kindergarten, I loved dressing up. Not in drag or anything – just fancy clothes. I was a big believer that clothes maketh the boy.

*

From about Year 1, I used to go fishing with Dad. Normally it was at dawn, not dusk as my poem 'Estuary at Dusk' suggests. We used to fish in front of the Tuross estuary boatshed and sometimes we would pull in twenty-something fish in a single session. We caught tailor, bream, flathead, trevally and flounder. Gurnards and toadfish were rarities. Sometimes Chris (our next-door neighbour) would come along.

*

Mrs Simpson was my Year 1 teacher. During class, I sang a bit of ABBA – 'money, money, money'. But she thought I was singing 'mummy, mummy, mummy'. Anyway…

*

Even in Year 2, if Mum was late in picking me up from school, I would cry. Normally I would catch the bus. But sometimes we arranged that I was to be picked up from school.

*

In Year 2, we had a dress-up parade. Luke and I had agreed to dress up as cavemen. I wore a robe and had a club which I brandished menacingly at onlookers (as did Luke). It was fun.

*

I remember my eighth birthday. I got a Transformer watch and an ice cream cake. I had asked Mum for an ice cream cake – not really knowing the practicalities of it – but, yes, there was such a thing. My class had it for afternoon tea.

*

At the end of Year 2, Dad called a family meeting. Mum had been offered a job in the public service and we were to relocate to Canberra the next year. Jen (my sister) would start Year 1 and I would start Year 3. It sounded good.

Years 3 to 6

In Year 3, I changed schools. I went from Moruya Public School in Moruya to Miles Franklin Primary School in Evatt, Canberra. My first real memory of Miles Franklin involves a play that some students (including me) put on. There was a stage where I was pretending to punch a boy but in the heat of the moment I actually hit him. When we finished the play, we had a laugh about that.

*

By Year 4, I was fully into rock music. I used to get up early of a Saturday morning and watch *Rage* and I also used to watch *Video Hits*. I used to love Poison. I also loved 'Sweet Child o' Mine' by Guns 'n' Roses and also 'Under the Milky Way' by the Church. I took an interest in the charts.

*

In Year 5, I was invited to a girl's birthday party but I didn't go. A number of girls held this against me and were looking for a way to vent their anger. So when I was having trouble with long division, they gave me shit about it, saying I had no brains at all (I was getting perfect marks for *Behind the News* essays). Anyway, it was horrible.

*

In Year 5, I had my first poem published in *The Canberra Times* – in the comics section! 'Dad's Cooking' was published on Sunday, 1 October, 1989. I even received a letter from the editor (Crispin Hull) and a cheque for five dollars. Here is the poem:

Dad's Cooking

I hate the way that my dad cooks.
Starving people wouldn't eat his food
if they knew how it looks.
He makes mashed potato go yellow.
It's the worst that you've ever seen.
He's really a very nice fellow,
but it's hard to forgive him when your
steak goes green.
Oh great, we're having takeaway,
I don't have to drown myself
in sorrow.
But I don't think I've got much of a
chance
of having takeaway tomorrow.

*

In Year 6, we had parliament. I was Prime Minister. I was head of the Power Party. To try to get elected, the head of each party made a speech. My speech was augmented by a song by Snap (a rap and techno group) which went, 'I've got the power'. Anyway, it worked. A mate of mine, Robert, was Leader of the Opposition. It was good fun.

*

In Year 6, I was hanging around with a boy named Jay. He spat in my hair. We got into a fight. I was facing him. I thought, I'll use my tae kwon do on him. I decided to use knife hand strike. But in the process of using knife hand strike, I poked him in the eye. Jay let out a horrible noise and hurried off to sick bay. Later, I found out he was okay.

*

In Year 6, I had a small part in the school production of *Joseph and the Amazing Technicolor Dreamcoat*. My part went, 'I know of a bloke in jail, who is hot on dreams, can explain old Pharaoh's tale'. Anyway, the director would always forget to thank me at the end of the show. That wound still festers!

*

In Year 6, I played rugby league for Miles Franklin. I was a winger. They never passed the ball to me. But I could tackle. Well, most of the time anyway.

*

On the last day of Year 6, I cried. Which is weird because I didn't really enjoy primary school all that much. A couple of people who were previously mean to me said goodbye to me, which was nice. I wondered what high school was like. Soon, I would find out.

Years 7 and 8

There were four boys from Miles Franklin Primary School who came to Canberra High in 1991: Paul, Jay, Robert and myself. I became really good friends with Paul. Paul, I, Robert and Jay hung around in the quadrangle at recess and lunchtimes. Then Robert and Jay went to join the popular people. Waterbombs and fruit would be thrown from one end of the quadrangle to the other (Year 7s versus Year 8s). One time, Paul got caught in the crossfire and copped a waterbomb to the groin. He started crying. 'I'm not crying, I'm laughing,' he said.

*

Paul and I were great mates. We would catch the same bus to school (we lived in the same suburb) and sometimes we would walk from the Belconnen bus interchange to Canberra High. We would stop for lollies along the way and sometimes I would tell Paul about *Fast Forward* (I loved sketch comedy) and we would have a laugh. Anyway, in my teens and twenties and some of my thirties, we had a bromance.

*

On 5 February 1992, Nirvana played the ANU Bar. It was an all ages show. A Year 7 boy in my tute group was going. I had a *Nevermind* cassette but I wasn't a huge fan. It took me until after Kurt Cobain's suicide to really get into them. Given the choice to go again, I would.

*

Soon after Robert and Jay left, Paul made friends with Greg, Adam and

Damon and a few others. I soon followed. Initially, things were good. I got along with Paul and those other boys. But soon they turned on me. It was fashionable to play *Streetfighter Two* with the boys after school. I played it but I wasn't very good (years later, I would complete it). I copped a lot of shit about that. It culminated in Adam kneeing me in the groin. The teasing got so bad I would have to go to sick bay during recess and lunchtimes. It was conveniently around the corner from where everyone hung out.

*

At the time, I had a red belt in tae kwon do (then it was brown, then black). This was a pretty good achievement for a fourteen-year-old boy. I was training three times a week and knew a number of patterns. But I knew I would have to break boards at a grading to get black belt. So I gave it up. But to quote my poem 'Tae Kwon Do', 'what I learned there – / discipline, determination, assertiveness, // I have taken with me and applied elsewhere'.

*

My sister was accepted into Radford (an Anglican, co-educational school) in Year 7 and there was an opportunity for me to enrol at the same time in Year 9. I thought about it a bit. Then I decided to let Mum know I was changing schools. It represented a fresh start where (hopefully) I wouldn't get bullied.

*

When I was in my early years of high school, I was an avid tennis player. Anyway. I wrote a prose poem about playing tennis called 'Friday Night Tennis'.

Friday Night Tennis

For two dollars you could get a burnt sausage with raw onion on tasteless white bread with cordial so heavily diluted it was difficult to determine what flavour it was. As often as you liked. And as many doubles matches as it was possible to fit in.

The man who ran it liked his tennis. Once, he was a linesman for a satellite tournament. A ball bounced near him and he felt obliged to drop it at the feet of the pro tennis player. The pro swotted the ball away. His pint-sized son grunted like Monica Seles when he hit his two-fisted backhand. Once, at the end of the night after watering the courts, he placed the nozzle of the hose facing the black night sky in the side netting. He turned on the tap. Water blurted out. He giggled hysterically.

His mother was a thin woman with fixed, curly hair and a nasal voice. I can remember her saying to her other son, 'Phillip, grab those balls!' Being adolescent and immature, Paul and I found this extremely funny. I still do.

Paul and I would stand on rickety play equipment and talk, while others would play a crappy game of French cricket or, worse, tips.

Then one of us would be called up to play a match. We would grab our balls and walk on to the stony, clay courts. Often beetles would drop from the hazy, white lights peering over the tennis courts. The beetles would lie on their backs and move their tiny limbs about. A kamikaze mission, I suppose, as most of them got trodden on by the truncated soles of tennis shoes. I tried to be humanitarian and flick them to the side, into the bushes.

At the end of the night, we would huddle together in the small clubhouse. The man who ran it would distribute prizes from Clint's Variety. I occasionally got a highlighter, or a grip, or a packet of chips. Then we would head out into the night to try and find our parents' cars …

*

That's all I remember about those nights. Or that's all I want to remember. But a few things stand out in my mind – the food, the people who ran it and most of all the beetles who would rather kill themselves than be part of Friday night tennis.

Year 9

I started my first semester of Radford in Year 9. A few weeks into my first semester, I was among a clique of boys sitting in an art class. One of the boys, Craig, began calling me derogatory homosexual slurs. He also mimicked my voice. Then, another of the boys, Emlyn, also taunted me. There was no way for me to deny it. I reacted to their taunts by withdrawing into myself. I was on the verge of tears. But I didn't want to give them the satisfaction of crying. Craig and Emlyn slapped hands as if my response was proof of how I was. It was horrible. They say some school teasing stays with you for the rest of your life. This has. At least I can take solace from what a psychiatrist later said to me – getting called a gay slur is worse if you are one.

*

I remember early on in Year 9 I had signed up for both debating and soccer. Soon I had to choose one or the other. I chose soccer. That was a mistake! I was hopeless at it. Or at least the majority of the team was really good. I didn't trouble the scorers much. Except when I volleyed the ball from about halfway in a game. It went up in the air and over the goalkeeper for a goal.

'That was a fluke, Byrne,' said Aidan, one of the team.

*

Also, a little into Year 9, I was playing soccer in the under 15 Radford boys team. We were playing Canberra Grammar. I was standing near the goals and a boy was marking me. He started shoving into me ceaselessly. I hadn't watched an AFL game at that stage – I didn't know the idea was to shove back. Anyway, I did nothing. Then the ball went back to the middle of the field.

Later, Craig said, 'You should have hit him.'

Simon, another boy, also said, 'You should have hit him.'

It was only Scott, a boy who ended up playing for the Australian indoor soccer team, who thought I did the right thing. 'You didn't give away a penalty. Great.'

*

Knowing that I would have art class on Monday, I spent all my weekend working on my homework drawing and also coming up with resistance that would stop the Craigs and Emlyns of this world in their tracks. Finally, it was the end of the lesson with only Craig and me left in the class.

Craig insulted me.

'What was that?' I said. 'I can't hear you when you talk out of your arse.' At least I had the satisfaction of saying that to him.

Craig began rag-dolling me. The matter was taken outside, where I eventually shrugged him off.

*

It was in Year 9 that I was first exposed to poetry in George Huitker's English class. I remember studying Robert Frost, Walt Whitman, Peter Skrzynecki and John Foulcher's 'Dawn Sounds' – which I loved. I had been asked to write poetry at Canberra High but I had never studied any. It was all new to me. It was pretty. I thought, yeah, I could do this…

*

The first two drafts of 'Estuary at Dusk' were written in Year 9. I showed a draft to George Huitker.

He said, 'This is very, very promising!'

But I didn't do anything with it until the holidays before my final year when I came close to finishing it.

Year 10

Craig and Emlyn weren't in my Year 10 art class but Dave was. Dave was good at art and ending up topping Year 10 art. Anyway, he was also a bodyboarder – as I was. Bodyboarders are kind of like surfers, except they lie down on their boards or get up on one knee and go across the wave. Anyway, Dave and I loved talking shop. There was to be no soccer competition that year. I knew Dave was a hockey player who had played in Year 8 and Year 9. I decided I would take up hockey and play in the same team as my mate Dave. But Dave said he was taking up basketball in Year 10. But playing hockey was fun even without him.

*

Playing hockey for Radford was awesome. For starters, unlike soccer, I was reasonable at it. I found a place at right half in the second XI. I wrote a poem called 'Hockey' which features an insight into my three years in the seconds. How 'we played the majority of games // on a synthetic grass / sand surface / which would leave a nasty graze // if you happened to trip over.'

*

The first time I went bodyboarding far out the back was in Year 10. I'd surfed Airport beach in Moruya, which was easy to get out the back. And I'd surfed the beach breaks of Tuross, including One-Tree closer to shore. But to get out the back at One-Tree was a bit more challenging. I did and caught a few waves. They were fun, two to four foot, and offshore.

*

Maths, science and English were all streamed at Radford in five classes. In Year 9, I was in third everything. But after two semesters in third science, I went up a class to second in Year 10 – based on a good knowledge of basic chemistry. But after a semester of second science, I went back down to third again. 'Get back to where you once belonged!' I said to Lachlan, a friend in third science.

*

In the second semester of Year 10, I took up cricket. I had never played before but liked the game. Reasoning that my wrist would be strong from playing tennis, I decided to be a leg spinner. In my first game, I took a sharp catch at cover. All the boys gathered around me. It was wonderful. It was even mentioned at the team meeting at training the following week.

*

My date for the Year 10 semi-formal was Jenni. She was really girly which I found attractive. We sat and talked at the semi-formal venue, the Boathouse, where I found out a bit more about her. She had a boyfriend who hit her. We were friends from there on in. We talked and I was sympathetic. Then we found out there was a semi-formal after-party. Before she left for it she hugged me. I didn't end up going to the after-party.

Year 11

At the beginning of Year 11, I would sit in the same spot at recess and lunchtime, just withdrawing into myself. None of the kids in my year paid much attention to me. I would sit hunched over, still as a statue. And sometimes I would sit round the side of the common room building doing the same thing. Eventually, a girl named Tiffany saved me from this solitude. We started hanging out.

*

In the second half of the cricket season, I was leg-spin bowling in the nets a lot better than in the first half. The Page oval near my house had nets and that summer I had gone there quite a bit. I just bowled at three stumps over and again. I sorted out my run-up, and I was a more accurate bowler because of the practice. When we travelled to St Pats at Goulburn, I was given a bowl.

Before I started bowling, I overheard one St Pats batsman say to the other, 'Have a look at his spin.'

In the first over, I went for two. Then in the next three overs I was straying onto the pads of this batsman who kept on pulling me. Eventually I ripped one and the batsman mistimed a shot and one of our boys, Joel, took the catch. It was the second-last delivery of the over. Then another batsman skied another one. Joel dropped a more difficult chance. I wasn't pissed off. It would have been a very good catch. I'll always remember my wicket, though.

*

It was on an Action bus that Tiffany and I agreed to start going out.

Tiffany was lovely. She was extremely bright; she did English, advanced maths extended, physics and chemistry. She helped me with maths and chemistry. In turn, I helped her with English a bit – which in Year 11 was my best subject.

*

I remember a night match playing for the Radford second XI hockey team. The other team had possession and one of the players was in the process of passing to another. I intercepted the pass. I looked up the field – there was no one, so I just ran as fast as I could and simultaneously dribbled the ball. I remember trying to cross it at the end of the field but I screwed it up and the ball went over the line. Anyway, the boys liked what I did nevertheless.

One of the boys, Ben, said, 'Pressure, Byrnesy, pressure.'

*

I was a decent hockey player, without being outstanding. I wasn't going to make the first XI in Year 11 but maybe Year 12. Anyway, I loved playing for the second XI. A guy in the first XI would sometimes, after watching the second XI play, tell me I played a good game. A goalkeeper in the second XI, who had played with me, said the same thing.

*

When I was seventeen, I wrote my first mature poem. It was called 'Omniscience'. It was about me at school – I wanted to be free. About that time, I decided that I wanted to be a poet. I entered 'Omniscience' in the Senior Poetry Section of the Radfordian Literary Awards. I received a commended award, which was okay. I decided to try to go one or two steps better (first or second prize), next year. Here is the final version of 'Omniscience', now called 'Volutions'.

Volutions

The globe showers light,
staining my face,
all scars are visible.
My world is timetabled
chaos, segmented into ruins.
I'm left hanging
like a spider
from frail threads,
or a droplet
questioning fate.
And I contemplate
ending my life.
Darkness covers
parts of my room,
contrasting with the light.
Shadows spilled over carpet,
edges etched on walls,
dark, forgotten corners…
I would rather people saw me
in the darkness
of a moonlit beach.
Letting go
of a spiral shell
and endless volutions.

*

In Year 11, I surfed at a particular river mouth on the NSW south coast on the way to Victoria. It was the best surf I ever had. Everywhere was just maxed out but this river mouth just had really hollow barrels. I remember pulling into one barrel and just getting swallowed. Then it started to rain. My mother and sister were waiting for me so I headed in. According to my poem 'The River Mouth', it was the best day of the year.

Year 12

On the first day of 1996, I wrote a poem called 'In the Near Future'. It was a futuristic vision of urban sprawl. It was conceptualised, in sixteen lines and in three stanzas. I thought it was a good size to be in *The Canberra Times* so I sent it to them. I waited a while, then I received a rejection slip from the literary editor. I worked on it some more.

*

In the holidays before Year 12, I took my poem 'Estuary at Dusk' and expanded it so it was two pages in length. I didn't normally work this way but the form necessitated it. It was about fishing. It was arranged in tercets (three-line stanzas) except for the first and last stanzas, which were quatrains (four-line stanzas). I showed it to Australian poet and teacher at my school, John Foulcher. He said, 'That's the best poem I've read by you so far.'

*

I broke up with Tiffany early in Year 12. It took me a while to let go. I spent some time in the library by myself, just reading poetry. But after a while I started hanging round a different coterie of friends – the common-room corner boys. This was a group of about ten boys who played a variety of sports. None of us were prefects. The only academic honour roll student amongst them was Sandy. Sandy went on to be a good mate of mine after school.

*

Maths was my worse subject. I remember changing from advanced maths to maths T at the start of the year. My new class was rowdy. I remember laughing in a class and not being able to stop. I had to go outside and laugh there.

*

In the first semester of Year 12, I was trying hard but doing poorly in all my subjects. I saw my GP, who suspected I had bipolar disorder and she referred me to a psychiatrist. My symptoms according to those who were there included depression, withdrawal from others, restlessness, agitation, poor concentration, confusion, anxiety and difficulty sleeping. I was given status for the first semester of year 12 and put on Prozac for a mood disorder. I took my first Lithium for bipolar disorder when I was twenty-one.

*

I struggled through maths T in my last semester. My final semester results were fortunate. I finished last out of all the students doing maths T. I got forty. But I got a D, not an E.

*

In my second semester of Year 12, I knew 'Estuary at Dusk' was my best poem and I knew I might win the 1996 *The Canberra Times* Young Writers Competition (college poetry) with it. So I entered it and it did. I gave John Foulcher the news in Modern Poetry Workshop, a class he took. He thought I was joking but when he learned it was the case he phoned me up and put a blurb about my win in the school newsletter. I received a certificate, my poem in *The Canberra Times* and $130 for my troubles. There was a prize ceremony, where I met the guy who came second – Josh. He liked Lewis Carroll as much as I did. Here is my finished poem:

Estuary at Dusk

The motor churns,
wavy patterns surfacing,
tiny breakers following
a boat ploughing over
the dead weight of water.
Other vessels are isolated
with the simple pleasures of fishing,
finding their own private cove
or island. Some stay, some drift
over the dark green depths.
The liquid skin skewered
by the beak of a pelican,
ripples of concentric circles…
The features of a boy
are caught in a reflection.
Green eyes gleaming
on a calm face, helping
to throw down the anchor,
for stability. He imagines
the flathead on the sand morass
or a series of tailor near
a line held taut by small digits.
A boy and his father
hauling a small catch
into the arch of the boat.
The foundation slapped
by contorting bream, trevally
and flounder whose heads are severed
on a brown chopping block.
The fish are bled in a canvas bag,
thrown over the side,

immersed in water.
Vermilion sunset,
darkness hooks the evening.
The motor starts again.
The bow planing over
swells of other boats.
A boy feeling
the spray on his cheek,
washing his face, falling
like rain on a windscreen.
His face cleansed
during tranquil summer evenings,
when the piquancy of fish
lingered on my skin.

*

In my second semester of Year 12, I submitted a portfolio (*Alphabet Soup*) of ten poems for Modern Poetry Workshop. For the portfolio, I got 15 out of 15. For the drafting of poems, I got 8.5 out of 10. Five poems from this portfolio – 'Volutions', 'In the Near Future', 'Estuary at Dusk', 'The River Mouth' and 'Tuross, 1984' – featured in *Estuary at Dusk: Poems 1995–2000*, my first book of poetry.

*

In my second semester of Year 12, I came second in the Senior Poetry Section of the Radfordian Literary Awards with 'Estuary at Dusk'. I had to receive the award from the principal at assembly. I walked on to the stage and I was beaming. I had also grown some facial hair in the days before Monday's assembly. I had the beginnings of a moustache and a goatee beard. I think the principal noticed but he didn't care. After all of the troubles I had had that year, I think he was just happy that I had won something (as I was).

*

I remember my last day at school. We had an assembly, and then the Year 11s sang a song – 'In My Life' by the Beatles. A lot of my year hugged each other and cried. But the common-room corner boys just strolled nonchalantly out of there. Craig was one of them. Over the holidays we began hanging out.

1997

I smoked pot with Craig once as a schoolboy. It was in 1996. I had one toke after a basketball game and laughed a bit. He phoned me up in January of 1997 and soon we were smoking pot regularly. My favourite and most honest poem that I've written about my experiences of pot smoking would have to be 'Living Dangerously'.

Living Dangerously

One summer,
I smoked a lot of marijuana.
We had just finished school,
Craig and I were rebelling
against the rigidness of it.
We would drive to the top
of a mountain, and look down
on the city, firmly believing
we were having more fun.
As Craig lit the bong
and I breathed in deeply,
it made a gurgling noise –
like coffee percolating.
Eyes glazed, we were high
as clouds, I felt light,
as though I was floating…
But I paid for it later –
with a wretched bout of depression,
which left me in bed, regretting
those reckless days.

*

I have also written poetry about 'my wretched bout of depression'. In the first half of 1997, I spent three months in bed. It was horrible – I wanted to sleep but I couldn't. I just lay there until my dad came home from work. I wrote a poem called 'Drowning' about my depression.

Drowning

In ninety-seven, when I was depressed,
long, deep sighs would emerge from my chest.
My good psych helped with my poor mental health,
I told Dad I thought of killing myself.
I looked at the twitching rabbits next door,
when Jill brought a gift I fell to the floor.
I spoke to Craig on the phone one more time,
exhausted at night I clocked off at nine.
Food was the only thing left that I liked,
I went floppy after my vein was spiked.
My jumbled head was full of talk
and I felt stiff when I would walk.
Tapes tried to relax me with serene speech,
I thought happiness had gone out of reach.
I was treading water below my head,
absconding from life, and drowning in bed.

Late in the depression, my psychiatrist put me on a new drug called Zyprexa, which worked wonders for me. As soon as I was well, I went over to Paul's house. Paul had been learning the guitar and we made up our first song, 'Haircut'. It was a simple song but catchy. Paul came up with the music and I came up with the lyrics.

*

Also, as soon as I was well, John Foulcher would look over my poems and make comments on them. One of the poems I showed him was a squib (a short, funny poem) called 'Opposites'.

Opposites

> When I was younger,
> at pre-school
> we learned opposites.
> A lady said to me,
> 'Hello, young man.'
> I replied,
> 'Hello, old woman.'

In July, I began voluntary work at the Belconnen Library. I would shelve fiction books. Afterwards, I would browse through their poetry section. Then I would find a book and read it, glimpsing sometimes at clouds and gulls through a nearby window.

*

In December, I was invited to the 1997 ANU Poets Luncheon. I submitted a poem to the selector – Michael Thwaites – which was accepted. It meant a free lunch (and wine) and my poem ('Tuross, 1984') in a booklet. I was to read my poem from the booklet. Michael Thwaites was also the convenor. After I read my poem, Michael made me read it again. I'd read it too fast. I didn't have much reading experience. I would've been nervous. Still, I enjoyed that day. It was being part of a tradition. Here is the poem:

Tuross, 1984

> In the shadows of Norfolk pines,
> we would reach up to the sky,
> to swing on branches.

Our skinny legs were whipped with needles
until the bus rolled over loose stones
in the lukewarm sunlight of morning.
My legs dangled from a vinyl seat
as we drifted down Allenby Road.
The bus radio was playing a Eurogliders song:
Heaven must be there
and it was,
captured in the clear music of the song
and the slow bus ride past scattered houses
in my first year of school.

1998

I attended first-year university in 1998. At the ANU, I began a Bachelor of Arts. In the first semester, I enrolled in an English unit (Introduction to Literary Study), a French unit (Introductory French 1), a History unit (Australian History), and a Sociology unit (Self and Society).

*

I was talking with a friend on the phone at the start of the university year. He said just check out the yellow seats outside the refectory – there might be Radford people there. So I socialised with a group of about twenty students from my school, mostly guys.

*

All my mates seemed to have part-time jobs. I maintained that my part-time job was poetry. In 1998, I wrote twenty-three poems. One of those was 'Waiting for the Mail'. It describes part of the process a poet goes through when he or she sends out poems to newspapers, literary journals and magazines.

Waiting for the Mail

I walk outside, to check
the mail. The screen door bumps
the latch a few times and stops.
It's a perfect spring day –
with lukewarm sunshine
sprayed on my back.

A feeble wind
brushes my shirt
and rustles the crinkled, papery leaves
on a nearby tree.
The house clamps shadows
on the grass. I hear the yawn of cars
on a nearby freeway and a melody
of bird calls. Butterflies flit their wings
in a flurry of activity.
I pry open the jaws
of the letterbox, its mouth empty.
It creaks
as it shuts, like a clam,
final, resolute.
I walk back inside
and peel back the blotched skin
of a soft banana
which turns to mush in my mouth.
Then, I hear the sputtering
of the postman's motorbike.
We greet, and he slaps the mail
on my palm. There's one for me –
good. I know it's about my poetry.
I hold my self-esteem in my hand.

I had some good fortune with the events in this poem. The motorbike comes on time and there is an envelope for me about my literary affairs. Ninety-eight was prolific in terms of my poetry. I was doing first-year university and I didn't have a part-time job. I was not on a mood-stabiliser and it made me feel quite creative.

*

In the first semester of my Arts degree at ANU, I received a Credit in my English unit, a Distinction in my French unit and a Credit in my Sociology unit. My History unit was a full-year one.

*

In the second semester of my Arts degree at ANU, I enrolled in an English unit (Introduction to Australian Literature), a French unit (Introductory French 2) and a Sociology unit (Contemporary Society). The History unit was ongoing.

*

I debuted in the local literary magazine *Blast* as a twenty-year-old. My prose poem, 'Darkness and Colourful Graphics', featured on page nine of issue thirty-eight.

Darkness and Colourful Graphics

On the third floor of the mall, off to one side, lurking, like a shadow spilled over everything, is a dark, coin-hungry arcade. I walk in to apply a critic's eye to this wasteland of electronics. Darkness smothers the arcade, punctured by florescent light. I walk around, disconsolately, amongst screens of colourful graphics. Thudding dance music is blaring.
Nine televisions are clumped together screening the video-clip of a disposable song.
A strobe sprays meagre light over a soft, felt pool table with balls stacked, like beads, inside it.
I hear a boy complain about a violent shooting game. And he's right – there's a temporary thrill and challenge, but there's nothing lasting about it – your money vanishes with each coin impulsively inserted into the slot.
Another guy begins the game – the violence is misleading – if

you shoot someone they shatter, like porcelain, and the pieces conveniently disappear.

Next, I observe a one-on-one fighting game that demands dexterity - to perform special moves requires a skilful manipulation of the joystick, and simultaneous pressing of buttons. It's hard – if you die quickly you're wasting your change.

Off to one side, an earlier form of entertainment, pinball machines – an enclosed diorama into which a ball is injected and slapped by mechanical flippers.

Nearby, a car racing simulation where a boy sits, and steers his vehicle which swerves and skids along a winding track, accelerating to phenomenal speeds.

I pass some old arcade games – ancient, simple, primitive compared to the sophisticated games of the present. It reminds me that we're always advancing.

I walk out, past a skill tester; a robotic claw that clutches at – but rarely plucks – soft, plush toys. It snatches the gullible. By shunning it, I realise I don't have the same faith in things any more as I once did. Once, as a child, I believed in anything.

*

In the second semester of my Arts degree at ANU, I received a Pass in my English unit, a Pass my a French unit, a Distinction in my Sociology unit and a Pass in my full-year History unit.

1999

In January, I attended the Wollongong Poetry Workshop at the University of Wollongong. Poems were written, redrafted, edited and read by poets. 1999 was the first year where it was decided to publish an anthology from the workshop. There were fifty-eight poets, including sixteen young poets attending from Hartwick College, upstate New York, USA. They were very curious about cricket. I remember, in a Wollongong pub, teaching some of the Americans the rudiments of the game and also the saying, 'It's just not cricket,' which they found amusing.

*

I continued with my Arts degree. At the start of the year, I enrolled in an English unit (20th Century Australian Fiction), another English unit (The Modern Novel into Film) and a History unit (Britain Explored). During the middle of the year, I got my grades from the first semester. For my first English unit, I got a Credit; for my second English unit, I got a Credit; for my History unit, I got a Pass.

*

During the middle of the year, I enrolled in another three units for my Arts degree. I enrolled in my first English unit for the semester (Eighteenth Century Literature), my second English unit (Empire and its Fictions) and a History unit (The Black and White Tribes of South Africa).

*

In September, I watched an AFL game. It was a preliminary final between Carlton and Essendon. It was the best football game I have ever seen. It had so many twists and turns. Carlton ended up winning by a point. I was a Swans supporter at the time. But the way Carlton played on the day converted me to their side.

*

In November, I was one of four poets selected by Geoff Page to contribute to a young poets paid reading at Chat's, a café on the ANU campus. I read five of my early poems.

*

During the reading, I read a poem called 'The Fauves'. Geoff had seen it previously and had advised me to change a line which read 'and separates hands from the stage'. 'I can't see it,' Geoff had said. So I changed it to 'at this small, crowded venue'. When I read that new line at Chat's, I looked up at Geoff. He liked it, as if there was an understanding between us. His look seemed to say, 'Well done, son.' Here is the poem:

The Fauves

After Violentine,
The Fauves take the stage.
We stand closer.
I'm on my third beer
and feeling mellow.
Their charismatic rock
further distancing us
from the thudding dance music
of Civic nightclubs.
We're like magnets
with opposing polarities.

Irrationality starts
with the mosh,
a bouncing frenzy
of bodies
that erupt
at this small, crowded venue.
Between songs, the band laughs and jokes,
a guy at the front of the crowd
keeps requesting songs,
now he is crowd surfing.
On his second go
he falls to the floor.
A fight starts in front of me
and is quickly stopped.
We head next door
to KC's virtual reality café.
Paul and Justin push coins
into Streetfighter EX.
They discuss finishing moves
while Brendan and I watch
the beautiful graphics
of death.
We leave the neon lights
and walk to the car.
Passing streetlights, a guitarist and a drummer
argue like a married couple.
It's two o'clock, I'm falling asleep,
remembering the crowd surfer
outside the Gypsy Bar
with a cut ear.
Perhaps he had the most fun,
I don't know.
I fall asleep, thinking
about energy, enthusiasm, life.

*

At the end of the year, I got my results for the second semester of the second year of my Arts degree. For my first English unit, I got a Credit; for my second English unit, I got a Credit; and for my History unit, I got a Pass.

*

In December, I was invited to the 1999 ANU Poets Luncheon. The theme was Afternoon De-Light. The poem that I read, 'Estuary at Dusk', loosely fitted in with this. I ate some food, drank some wine, talked to some poets and was part of a tradition.

2000

At the start of the year, I began keeping a diary – something that I've kept doing up until this day. I was going for lots of bike rides, watching some tennis and playing chess against Paul. Also, I was writing my sketch comedy series, sending out poems to journals and trying to get my band together.

*

I briefly attended ANU in early 2000. I was two-thirds into an Arts degree and I was doing two English units, a History unit and a Sociology unit. I was manic (having elevated mood) but not really aware of it. I was behaving strangely. It all started when I went off Prozac and Zyprexa (an antipsychotic) and went on sleeping pills instead. I wanted to join the army reserve and they would not allow soldiers to take antidepressants and antipsychotics.

My psychiatrist said, 'Take two sleeping pills, then one, then none.'

*

For three nights, I got some sleep. Then one night I couldn't get to sleep at all. I took six sleeping pills and I still couldn't get to sleep. I phoned my psychiatrist. 'Manic depression is a frustrating mess,' I said.

'I know,' said my psychiatrist.

*

After behaving strangely at university, I decided to go see my psychiatrist. What happened is documented in my poem 'My First Lithium'.

My First Lithium

I was twenty-one, and high and mighty.
I stomped to my psychiatrist, angry.
I took a seat, felt better, turned mellow.
I went in, happy as a child in snow.
Then I asked him for an arm wrestle,
got turned down. I began to whistle
and asked the man where he went to school
as if it mattered, where there were rules
and always someone aberrant to break them.
I had become much more interesting again.
I sang happy songs to a portrait, a windowsill.
He turfed me out, gave me water and a bitter pill
to swallow, like the diagnosis, a habit I had to keep.
Something I never had before, but needed, like sleep.

*

With that, I withdrew from university for the semester.

*

Just before my twenty-second birthday, I had a jam session with Paul and another guy named Peter. I had met Peter at the Belconnen bus interchange. He had a guitar with him and we swapped contact details. I phoned him up numerous times to arrange a jam session with him, a drummer and a bass player. Now, having an acoustic session with just Paul, Peter and myself was not really what I was after. But it was an okay compromise after about four months of organising.

*

I met Paul and Peter at the Florey shops and we walked home. Back at my place, Peter got out his acoustic and strummed on it. Then Paul played 'Love You' then 'Us'. We got through two-thirds of 'I Loved Her' then Paul got sick of playing power chords and had a pineapple juice. He played three more songs then we workshopped one song that wasn't quite finished. Then we watched video clips, including one song by Joy Division which I thought we could cover.

*

After the jam session, Peter told me our songs were okay (we didn't have anything good at this stage) but his old band Guff were reforming. Plus he said he jammed with two other guys. And that was that. Although I phoned him up a few times during the rest of the year, just to see what he was up to.

*

The day after my twenty-second birthday, I went bowling with Thomas. Thomas got 66 in his first game and 91 in his second. I bowled a 108 then a 111. Then we went to Sails, where I had two beers. Thomas had a beer and a coke. We drove for a while.

I was still a little drunk. I pointed at a zebra crossing near my bicycle. 'Drop me off at the happy walk,' I said.

*

From May to June, I did voluntary work for the Belconnen Library. It was mainly shelving. The person in charge of me, Cathy, said I was the library's most reliable volunteer. I've done about a year's worth of voluntary work at the Belconnen Library. The last time I worked there was in 2008.

*

I went and saw Mental as Anything in early May with Sandy (I can't remember where). They played all the classics. Sandy didn't really know all the songs but I still think he enjoyed it.

At the end of their set, one of them asked, 'Any requests?'

'Rock and Roll Music,' I yelled out.

'Does anyone know any Chuck Berry?' one of them said.

*

In July, I went away with my family to Port Macquarie. I went bodyboarding there at Flynn's Beach. It was crowded but I managed to catch half a dozen waves one day, including my last wave, which was a long wall ending in a closeout section. I saw one guy getting barrelled – I looked at him in the pit and just smiled at him.

*

I went back to uni in the second semester of 2000. I did an English unit called 16th, 17th and 18th Century Literature and a Sociology unit called Sociology of Third World Development. The idea was to ease my way back into my studies.

*

Earlier on in the year, I had met a young woman named Dee. She was doing development studies at ANU. I met her at the poetry at Bazaart. I went on one date with her. I told her about my bipolar disorder. She said it sounded like fun before I told her about the depression part.

*

Lyn was a woman I met when I was doing my first paid reading at Chats Café in 1999. Lyn was a Radford girl in the year two years ahead of me (class of '94). I asked her out on a date but she was engaged to someone else. Not a poet, though, she told me.

*

In October I got a poem 'A Memory of Tuross' in *The Canberra Times*. I was twenty-two and it was my biggest publication to date. I was paid fifty dollars for it. It was the culmination of a lot of hard work.

A Memory of Tuross

In my early years of adolescence,
I got out of the water
at One-Tree beach, numb with cold.
I smothered myself
with a towel. Then we went for ice creams.
I remember it
oozing out of the machine,
making a winding tower
that I polished with my tongue –
working away at it, like a cat
licking its paws, before I bit
into the bland, brittle cone.
The ice cream and the calm stillness
of the estuary combined to uplift me.
This, I knew, was paradise.

I achieved a Credit in my English unit and a Credit in my Sociology unit in my university studies. I looked forward to next year. I had six units to go.

2001

Early on in the year, I spent two weeks in Victoria. The first week my parents and I went camping on a farm near Elmore (near Bendigo). Then we stayed in Melbourne for a week. We went to the Australian Open tennis tournament and saw Mary Pierce, Roger Federer, Pat Rafter and Marat Safin. In a night match, I saw Andre Agassi and the lovely Anna Kournikova. Being myself, I stood out in crowds.

*

In February, I had an offer to publish my poetry manuscript from Ginninderra Press. I was to put my poems on a disk as soon as I was able. It felt wonderful.

*

In February, I bought a bass guitar and a practice amp. This was good, as I had already had a couple of bass lessons without a bass. It was a good bass guitar – a Fender Squire and a Fender amp also.

*

I started off the first semester of my studies doing three units: an English unit called 19th and 20th Century Poetry, a History unit called World at War, 1939–1945 and a Sociology unit called Classical Sociological Theory.

*

From March to May, I was questioning whether I wanted to continue with university. This impinged on my mental state. There was lots of pacing, confused thinking and difficulty in sleeping.

*

Paul and I taped 'Daily Grind'– a song that we had just written. It was the best song we had so far. I showed Paul this song that I had written but he didn't like it. But he took one section of it and expanded on it. I wrote some lyrics for it which had a whinge about university. It took me a while to learn it on the bass. It had seven parts but it was the most enjoyable song to play out of the ones we'd written.

*

That semester, I got a Pass (56) in my English unit. If I had achieved a Credit, I would have been right for Honours. I missed out on honours by four per cent. I also achieved a Pass in History, and a Credit in Sociology.

*

In semester two, I did three units: a unit of English titled American Accents, Race, Gender and Ethnicity in Modern American Literature; another unit of English called Contact Discourse (which I was student representative for); and a History unit called The American Sixties.

*

In late July, I read 'Howl' by Allen Ginsberg in the Chifley Library (I was writing an essay on Ginsberg's poetry for my History unit). I loved 'Howl' and read the poem in one sitting. I loved the beginning, 'I saw the best minds of my generation destroyed by madness.' Madness I could relate to.

*

In late September, I had a conversation with Stephen Matthews (the publisher at Ginninderra Press). He said the book could be out by early December. I needed to give him the revised proof of the manuscript and to find a cover for it. Then I would look at the final proof before it would take two weeks to get printed. The front cover consists of pelicans cruising on the Tuross estuary. I took the shot. The title was to be *Estuary at Dusk: Poems 1995–2000*. The 'estuary at dusk' part was to do with the title of the best poem in the book (I thought) – 'Estuary at Dusk'. The 'poems: 1995–2000' part was do with the arrangement of a lengthy fifty-two poems into four sections.

*

For the last semester of my Arts degree, I got a Credit in American Accents, a Distinction in Contact Discourse and a Credit in The American Sixties. The result I was most pleased with was History. I had never achieved above a Pass in my History units and to get a Credit was a nice way to finish.

*

The book launch of *Estuary at Dusk: Poems 1995–2000* went well. It was held at the University of Canberra Co-op Bookshop. The boys from next door came, George Huitker (my Year 9 English teacher) came, Thomas showed up with his girlfriend, Paul came late (better late than never), Jen (my sister) and Justine (her friend) were there, Mum and Dad came, plus Jill (my aunt) and her friend Mary came along. And of course there was my friend Bill Tully, who launched the book. Bill made a substantial speech, commenting on adolescence as well as paying close critical attention to a few of the poems. My speech wasn't perfect in the delivery (I was nervous). I stumbled three times – my voice was fine but my hands were shaking. But the reading of my poems was flawless. When signing books, the usual message was 'all the best'. Also, Justine blew me a kiss before she left with Jen. Then we kicked on at the Rubicon, a Canberra restaurant.

With my bear Bruno.

My lovely mum holding me.

From left: cousins Greg and Rochelle and me at Tuross.

With my sister Jen.

The photo from the front cover of Southbound, *my second book of poetry.*

Dress-ups: My sister as the old woman who lived in a shoe, me as a caveman.

Me and my friend Robert off the Tuross boat shed.

From left: cousins Anita and David, Jen and me.

Me sporting a Prince racquet and a Mizuno shirt.

Just before a tae kwon do grading – in which, hopefully, I would go up a grade.

At Canberra High School.

My family.

From left: cousins Greg and Rochelle, Jen and me.

Jen, my mum and me on the balcony at Tuross.

My mate Luke playing table tennis with me.

Jen and me in our Radford College blazers.

From left: Jen, my paternal grandmother and me.

My maternal grandparents.

My parents.

With Celtics cap, Rusty shirt and HB board at Airport Beach, Moruya.

Pulling into a wave.

Me and my friend Paul with fish we caught in 1996.

My dad, a living legend.

With Dad on the Mount Dromedary trail, bonding.

My sister and I sporting rock music T-shirts.

With Jimi Hendrix T-shirt.

At Poet's Point, reading to Bill Tully (left), Mr Light (right) and others.

Pensive, with a fern in the background.

Doing a paid reading at Mount Majura Vineyard, 2009.

The cover photo from A Man of Emails, *my third book of poetry.*

Jen holding her baby Avery while her partner Jane looks on.

Me holding Avery. I had never held a baby before.

Dad, Mum and I (with a Carlton tie and designer stubble).

My lovely sister Jen.

Reading at the launch of New & Selected Poems *at Paperchain Bookshop, Manuka, 2014.*

2002

In the first semester of 2002, I enrolled in a Graduate Diploma of Education at the University of Canberra. I was determined to become a high school English and History teacher. I studied there full time, enrolling in Education Foundations, Information Technology and Education, Promoting Positive Learning Environs, Secondary Teaching Studies and Professional Experience.

*

In late January, there was also a picture and article about me in *The Moruya Examiner*. It was basically a plug for *Estuary at Dusk*. There was a 'strong flavour of Tuross' about it and I had 'strong links, and feelings for Tuross'. I would take my 'Diploma in Education course in Canberra this year' and I hoped 'to go on to a career in teaching secondary students'. It was my first book but not my last.

*

In February, *Estuary at Dusk* was reviewed in *The Canberra Times*. I was demonstrably learning my craft 'as a poet'. My collection 'includes thoughts about that most unlikely of subjects, the *Super Mario Bros 3* electronic game'.

*

In March, I did a stand-up routine in a *Raw Comedy* heat. Sandy was there and patted me on the back before I went on. I only got one laugh in a five-minute set. Looking back on it, I was manic (having elevated mood). I got through it okay, though. A few years later, I would try stand-up again before shelving it completely.

*

In March, I did a reading in Canberra which went well in front of one of my poetry mentors, Geoff Page. I was determined to read well in front of Geoff because I knew he could get me another paid reading if he thought I was good. He also had critiqued some of my poems which I had given to him and he gave them back at the reading. When asked how come none of my friends were there for the reading, I replied, 'They've all got part-time jobs.'

*

I did Professional Experience (practising teaching) at Canberra High School in March. There were only two teachers that were there when I was a student at the school – the principal and Mr Osmond (a PE teacher who had taught me in the early nineties). I mixed with other teachers in the staffroom. When asked to introduce myself, I said, 'I'm Michael Byrne, otherwise known as Mr Byrne.'

*

In April, I went for a walk after getting nowhere with some computer stuff. I came back and told Dad I was quitting uni. We discussed some pros and cons until he suggested going part-time and I agreed. It meant dropping Information Technology and Education, Secondary Teaching Studies and Professional Experience, but that was okay.

*

One of the most harrowing days of my life occurred on 'Black Friday'. My psychiatrist had put me on Valium and I needed a prescription. It was pissing down rain and I was manic and I'd only had about four hours' sleep. I was frayed at the edges. My goal was to get a Valium prescription. I phoned up my psychiatrist's secretary and requested one to be given to me that day. I found out I had to wait fifteen minutes to get my confirmation that the Valium was coming. I became impatient, jumped ship and called about half a dozen psychiatrists as well as my GP (I got her answering machine) as well as a psychiatrist in Lyneham who recommended I go to the Florey Medical Centre. So I stomped there in the wet. By this stage I was angry.

I walked into the Florey Medical Centre. 'I want a Valium prescription, now!' I said.

'You'll have to wait and pay forty dollars,' said the woman at the desk.

'For fuck's sake!' I said and stormed out of there, the rain still pissing down.

I headed back home and called my psychiatrist. He had arranged for me to get the script. I walked through the pissing rain to the mall. As I got into the mall, I felt this weird aura as if I was going to faint, or have a seizure or a heart attack or a panic attack. On an escalator going from the third floor to the second, I was advised by a couple to sit down. So I did for a while. Then I walked through the mall in tears and by the time I got to the car park I was howling and sobbing uncontrollably. I did the same on the bus. The bus driver gave me his condolences and I trudged up to Calvary Hospital. I was still crying when I got to my psychiatrist's rooms. His secretary gave me three glasses of water. I saw my psychiatrist briefly. My mother drove me home.

Oh, and I got the Valium prescription.

*

In July, I went with my family to Pacific Palms on the north coast for a week. I had to kick Valium, and I warned my family I would have side effects from it. I was also manic. I fought with my parents a bit. On the plus side, I had some good surfs. For my last surf, I surfed the shore break at Boomerang and got about fifty waves. It was one of the better surfs I've had. I even did an aerial off a right, which I'd never done before.

*

I got a Credit in Education Foundations and a Pass in Promoting Positive Learning Environs in my Graduate Diploma of Education for my first semester. However, I lasted a week in the second semester before giving it away.

*

However, in the second semester I met a young woman. She had been in my Education Foundations tute and she had made a good impression on me. She was in my tute in the first week back and we got talking. After the tute, I asked for her phone number and she asked for mine. She called me late at night on a Saturday. She told me on Sunday when I returned her call that she wanted to go out. We talked on the phone a few more times and then I went to see her in person.

*

The best way I can communicate what happened on my first date with this young woman is to incorporate a prose poem.

An Evening in the Life

Late afternoon. He dodged around students, a smooth poetry book in his hand to read selectively from for the duration of the tute. He hunched against a wall, intermittent words filtered through a shut door. During a break halfway through the tute, he smiled at her apprehensively and suggested they do something afterwards. His eyes flickered over some poems and he drew some basic outlines of faces. The tute finished, he shoved his hands into his pockets and they left the building together.

She led him downstairs into a thinly populated bar. They talked for a while, nervously. She kindly offered to buy him a beer, but he declined. She went and a got a drink, bubbling excitedly to the person who got her a beer. An older male friend of hers joined them, who talked enthusiastically about sex. It made the younger man feel uneasy. The older man flicked through the poetry book of the younger man, which he had given her as a gift. She knocked back three more beers. As she placed her fourth on her coaster, the younger man got worried. He curtly told her it was her last, but this curtness was a kind of love. She mentioned she knew some guy from a show on television. He said that they had spoken about him on that show once or twice.

Towards the end of the evening, he asked her if he could sleep on her couch. It made sense to him – he didn't have a car and he wasn't sure how well her drunk friend could drive. He could catch a bus with her, and, well, sleep on her couch. He was tired, and it would be better walking home a similar distance in the lucidity of daytime. She said the people she lived with wouldn't appreciate that. He then shook her hand, awkwardly. She smiled, politely, as she disappeared with her friend. He veered to leave one way, reconsidered, then headed out the other side.

He stepped into the dimly lit dark, and was crucified.

*

In late August, I was hospitalised for four days. I spent one night in the public psychiatric ward 2N before being transferred to Hyson Green. I met some bipolar sufferers for the first time. Almost everyone just sat outside and smoked in the wintry sun. I smoked one cigarette and didn't have another.

*

In mid-September, I went on another date with this young woman. What happened is best captured in a prose poem.

A Date

A mutual gathering of friends. It sends me delirious. I want to impress you – a nineteen-forties screen siren, star-struck, in need of bucks. But what I do does not entertain you and how I come across is not as funny as Bros. Before this event, I'm excited as a kid before Christmas and consequently no sleep and I'm too busy with plans for me to count sheep. And when we get there our problems are poured into the air. They leave me forlorn as a lamb and this is not going to work out and I'll go back to where I started from and I don't want you to hurt me but it seems as if you already have.

*

In December, I went to read some poetry at Toast (a nightclub in the centre of Canberra). But mostly it was musicians playing. I could have left, but I decided to just stay in a corner and watch people. I enjoyed this. I became a fly on the wall, a voyeur.

*

My family spent Christmas day with the Hansons (relatives of ours). We ate, talked, laughed and drank and then they left. Afterwards, my dad encouraged me to have a couple more beers. As I was doing so, the conversation suddenly turned to Vietnam and Dad (a Vietnam veteran) started crying. I'd never seen Dad cry before. My sister told him that he never talked about it and that he should. Dad said I'd been good over the last four months. He also said he didn't care what I did as long as I was happy.

2003

At the start of 2003, I began a Masters in Journalism (externally) from the University of Wollongong. To enter the course, I had to have maintained a Credit average in my undergraduate degree. I had achieved that. I also had to have had at least a dozen items of writing published. I had achieved that with my poetry. On the strength of my poetry, I had the opportunity to undertake the course. In the autumn session, I enrolled (part-time) in News and Feature Writing as well as On-Line and Research Journalism.

*

In January, I got a call from my Aunt Jill. She notified me that there was a bushfire alert in Canberra. I listened to the radio, but the suburb of Florey (where I lived at the time) was never threatened by the bushfires. Considering what happened, I was lucky to live where I lived.

*

In March, I talked to Lachlan Coventry on the phone for the last time before he went overseas. Lachlan was a good friend. What I liked about Lachlan was that he was good at being serious or humorous. Also, his selflessness. He phoned me up one time and told me John Kinsella (a poet I liked) was reading on an ABC arts show. I was grateful for that.

*

In April, I was hospitalised for five days. I was feeling suicidal and couldn't concentrate on my university work.

*

In June, I had a poem, 'At the Library' in *Blue Dog* (a literary journal). I received a copy of *Blue Dog* in the mail and a cheque for forty dollars for the poem. I drafted it a bit more after it was published.

*

I got a Credit in News and Feature Writing as well as a Pass in On-Line and Research Journalism. I also enrolled in my two units for my next semester of study. They were Journalistic Method and Practice as well as Ethics, Law and Standards.

*

I spent eleven days in hospital in August. It was around this time I started hearing voices, male and female voices, which were commenting on me. It felt like I was constantly being observed. I later wrote a poem called 'The Voices'.

The Voices

Two voices exist
outside my head,
if I leave the house
or go to bed
they do not exist.
But they are here now,
passing judgements,
they do not allow
me freedom
from being observed,
I have no privacy,
I do not deserve

these voices. Like an animal
in a domestic zoo,
I feel like an exhibit.
Like what I say or do
is being criticised,
but they are in the wrong.
Last night, my stereo
played raw and angry songs
to ward them off
but they came back
offended and hurt,
on the attack.
There is no pleasing them
and what they say
filters into a mind
starting to fray.
I have stepped outside
in the night and the day
and heard reassuring silence
and I wish it would stay.
But stubbornly
the two voices come back
like bad nightmares,
like past affairs,
or advancing soldiers
on the attack.
These voices
will not go away.

*

In October, Sandy came round to my place. We walked to the Ginninderra Tavern and had two beers each. We talked about various stuff –

sport, making mattresses and braces. Then we walked home and he headed off. I absolutely loved those nights I spent drinking with him.

*

In December, I went to a poetry reading at Red Belly Black Café. A woman named Veronica asked me to email 'Coming Back' (one of my poems) to her. I did. She sent me back an email saying she liked my poetry and that she was a depressive herself (I told her I was a manic-depressive). That was the beginning of our correspondence.

*

In my second semester, I got a Pass in Journalistic Method and Practice as well as a Distinction in Ethics, Law and Standards.

2004

At the start of 2004, I enrolled in Print Production and Publication as well as Directed Readings in Journalism as part of my Masters in Journalism degree.

*

I knew I had a reading in April. I was going to be one of four poets to read at Red Belly Black Café as part of the first New Voices Reading. For my previous reading in 1999, I didn't rehearse it beforehand. I made a few mispronunciations. So, this time around, I rehearsed the reading a few times.

*

My reading went fine. I made two mispronunciations but that was okay. I allow myself three or less. Veronica came to the poetry at Red Belly Black. She was a librarian, four years older than me and smart and attractive. At the end of the reading, she took me to a spot overlooking the city and we talked. Then we walked back to her car and she dropped me home.

*

That weekend, Veronica came around to our place. She gave me the cheque that I had left in her car. We went for a drive out to Bungendore, where she bought a Norman Lindsay lithograph. We also went to the woodwork place, where I had a lemonade and she a milkshake. I found her to be both deep and kind. I thought I came across all right – I made a few jokes and said some erudite stuff. We hugged at the end. I felt I had a basic grounding of who she was.

*

In April, I watched some television that I thought had had a go at me. I felt so bad that I tried to kill myself. I listened to 'Tuesday' by You Am I which got me in the mood. I listened to 'In Utero' by Nirvana after I wrote my suicide note then I had six beers, six Prozac, six Zyprexa and eight Epilim. It didn't even put me to sleep. Mum came into my room. After hearing me talk, she took me to the hospital, where I stayed overnight. I had the week off uni and applied for special consideration.

*

I achieved a Credit for Print Production and Publication as well as a Credit for Directed Readings in Journalism. Considering I had a hospitalisation and a suicide attempt, I thought it was a good effort.

*

In July, I received a letter from Stephen Matthews about the manuscript for my second book. I was to meet him and Bill Tully (a friend) for a chat in Civic at 1.30 p.m. I did so. They gave me some feedback on the manuscript and a free milkshake. Stephen showed me the poems that didn't work and I showed him some new poems like 'Words' and 'Schizoaffective Disorder' which he liked. He also wanted me to put the poems into sections. That was fine with me.

*

In August, I found out I had 'Schizoaffective Disorder' in *The Canberra*

Times. It was (and still is) one of my best sonnets. It was the third poem I had published in *The Canberra Times* after 'A Memory of Tuross' and 'Coming Back'. It felt good.

Schizoaffective Disorder

Being killed by kids on crowded buses.
Schizoaffectiveness has no pluses.
Children can hunt your emotions for sport
when the grim graveyard of your mind
is dug up, and the rules of school
are then carried onto public transport.
Thus a young girl becomes unkind,
thus a young girl hurls ridicule.
Her taunts linger like a note off key.
I express the hurt repressed in me.
I sit and sigh, devoid of speech.
The truth for her is beyond reach.
As the bus hisses at my fingers,
the graven ghost of her spite lingers.

*

I enrolled in International Journalism and Multicultural Journalism as part of the last semester of my Masters in Journalism.

*

In October, I received a message from Stephen Matthews at Ginninderra Press saying he would publish the book (called *Southbound*) in its new form. He wanted me to put the poems on a disk. I was glad Stephen would publish the book in the form it was now in. With the title, when someone says he or she is heading south, a meaning is that the person is heading in a bad direction. This pertained to me at the time. Another meaning pertaining to me is that I'm bound to the south – the south coast of New South Wales which is my spiritual home.

*

In November, I went to the second New Poets reading in Yarralumla (Beess & Co). Veronica was there. After the second reading, we went outside. I asked her if she wanted to be more than just friends. She told me she'd been seeing a guy for seven or eight years. I would make the effort to contact her but I was unsure how she would respond.

*

In November, I found out I had Credits in International Journalism and Multicultural Journalism. Thus I had completed my Masters Degree. I had a glass of wine with my parents.

*

In November, Veronica put me in contact with a woman from her work – Rosemary. I sent her a couple of emails and she sent me a couple.

*

In December, I took Rosemary on a date to the poetry at Yarralumla (Beess & Co). We talked for a while and then I told her I was a bodyboarder. I said if I was fit enough, I would surf Shark Island (a notorious reef break in Cronulla). Rosemary was most impressed (she was from Cronulla originally). It was a good move!

*

I'm so glad our date went well. My last date was in 2002 and that was awful. But this time I had the advantage of a sound mind.

*

One night in December, Rosemary gave me a ring. She wanted to have a chat. She was dropped off at my place about 9.45. We went for a walk to the Page oval. The conversation went really well.

*

In December, I went bowling with Rosemary and her friends. Then we went to Zeffirelli's to have pizza. I bowled in one lane with Rosemary and her friends bowled in another lane. I bowled a 97 and a 116. Then Rosemary drove me over to Zeffirelli's. I had a satay chicken pizza and some garlic bread. I spent the night talking to Tara (verbose and offbeat) and Carmen (surly but funny). I had fun.

2005

One of the first jobs I applied for was a graduate position with the Office of Indigenous Policy Coordination. I was informed that I was to attend an assessment centre. I had a ten-minute presentation in front of three people. One of them asked me what my weaknesses were. I replied, 'I don't have any.' Fortunately, they laughed.

*

In January, I invited Rosemary around for a game of chess. At the end of the night, I tried to kiss her but she refused, then hugged me, then left. I didn't hear from her for a week. Then we emailed for a while and then lost touch.

*

I bought my first car in January. It was a white '98 Nissan Pulsar SLX. Dad helped me pick it out.

*

I knew Steve Kelen from the Canberra poetry scene. He was a really good poet as well as an intelligent and sensible guy. I came to know him better when he wrote an imprimatur for *Southbound* (my second book of poems). Then I suggested we become friends. After some deliberation, we decided on tennis as an activity we could do together.

*

In March, I launched my second book of poems – *Southbound*. Geoff Page turned up, so did George Huitker. Steve Kelen couldn't make it. But Robert Murphy (a friend of my family) did and his girlfriend and friend. Stine (a friend of my sister) showed, as did Row (also a friend of my sister) and her partner. My sister turned up with Banks (her girlfriend). Finally, my cousin Greg turned up. I read four poems and only made one mispronunciation.

*

In July, *Southbound* was reviewed by Professor Peter Pierce in *The Canberra Times*. Pierce died in September 2018. He was an academic, editor and literary critic. According to Pierce, there was 'manifest intelligence' in my poetry and 'an emerging technical competence'. He finished with 'let us hope for more from him'. A good review.

*

In October, I did an unpaid reading at M16 – an art gallery near the Fyshwick Markets in Canberra. There were about fifty people there for the reading. I checked the visual art out, bought a brownie and ate it with a couple of people and mixed with other people before my reading. I read 'The Death Knell', 'The Hallowed House of Nevermind' (an outtake from my next book – *A Man of Emails*) and 'The Similes and Metaphors Alone'. Then I gave a few copies of *Estuary at Dusk* away, saying, 'The best things in life are free.'

*

In October, I had a column published in *The Canberra Times*. My column, 'The highs and lows of a manic life', was published in *Front Up* (a forum for young people). A copy of this column is included in Artciles and Reviews. In it, I explain about how I suffer from schizophrenia and bipolar disorder and the symptoms and traits of these illnesses.

*

In 2005, I had four job interviews for graduate positions. I wasn't successful in getting one.

*

On a brighter note, in 2005, I played six sets of tennis with Steve and won three.

2006

In January, I floated to Stephen Matthews the idea of an anthology to help celebrate Ginninderra Press's tenth birthday. I proposed to him that I do the anthologising. He thought it was a great idea and was willing to help. Soon enough, fifty poets that I was to anthologise gave me permission to use their poems. Stephen suggested I proffer a number of possible titles for him. Then he chose one of my lines – 'On common water'. The line was taken from my poem in the anthology – 'Ode to Breakwalls'.

*

In March, I was still corresponding with Veronica. I phoned her, requesting for her not to ditch me. I said she was beautiful, wise, intelligent and funny. She seemed to like that, because she sent me an email the next day.

*

In March, I had a column, 'Pub poetry reading just like old times', published in *The Canberra Times* (see Articles and Reviews).

*

By April, I was manic (having elevated mood). I had no inhibitions at all. I remember talking to a young woman at the shops who was smoking a cigarette. I just walked up to her and scammed one. Then we went into the chemist and she bought something and I bought some cough medicine. Then we parted ways.

*

In April, I went to a RSVP singles night. I met a woman – Anna. She was twenty-six, and ran a health clinic. She was also a dance instructor. She gave me her mobile number and her email address. I sent her an email and soon after went to her dancing class. But Anna was too good to be true. She was just drumming up business for her dance classes.

*

Nevertheless, the RSVP singles night went really well. I wore some cool threads, stayed longer, did some flamboyant dancing, drank two beers and eschewed the 'chicken dance'. The DJs played some great songs from bands I hadn't heard in ages like the Choirboys and the Screaming Jets. Then I went home and watched *Rage*.

*

Sometimes, when you're manic, you feel invincible. You can be brave to the point of being foolhardy. Which was the case with me on Easter Sunday, 2006. Amongst some surfers, I was checking out the surf at Airport Beach. It was totally maxed out but I still insisted on going for a surf. I duck-dived under the swells and found myself out the back. I tried catching one of the waves but they were reforms that were breaking way further in. Not only that; I was in a rip. I tried climbing up the rocks of the breakwall, but the swell got me. A plane droned overhead. By this stage, I was keeping in touch with two men on the breakwall.

'Swim out of the rip,' one of the men said.

I tried but could not. By this stage I was getting tired.

Then one of the men clambered down the breakwall and perched on a rock above the water. I paddled over to the man and he grabbed my arm. As he pulled me up, my board scraped on the rocks and I got a few cuts on my legs too. But I was in one piece and I had my board.

My next instinct was to warn all the surfers that there was nothing out the back. Then I came back and thanked the man for rescuing me.

'Just have an egg and a beer and you'll be right.' he said.

'I'll have a beer,' I said.

*

After my near-death experience, I sat in the car by myself. The car stereo was playing 'Six Months in a Leaky Boat' by Split Enz. I just lost it, broke down completely.

*

In May, I attended the Canberra book launch for my anthology – *On Common Water*. But the Sydney book launch I had to turn down – I was too high to go. I included my own poem 'Ode to Breakwalls' in the anthology.

Ode to Breakwalls

> Breakwalls are like an upturned middle digit
> against nature, fixed prisms surfers crave.
> On common water they jostle and fidget
> before tacking into waves, seeking caves.
> Refraction of the swell is the attraction.
> The surfboard riders voice their predilection
> as the inside low tide hang glide section
> barrels, before the next set provides action.
> These locked rocks, this compacted cereal.
> Man made refractor of the ethereal,
> warping waves collapsing on flanks of banks.
> Surfers paddle out as their local cranks
> while off the breakwall fishermen angle
> observing the scene as their lines dangle.

*

By May, I was a smoker. I started off with Marlboro Reds. Then I smoked Alpines, Marlboro Lights, Holiday Kings, Holiday Slims, Longbeach and Stuyvies.

*

By May, I was hospitalised with mania for eleven days. I became friends with a Marist boy, Eamon (a cutter), and Brad (a depressive schoolboy). And what was I? The schizophrenia didn't even enter into it. I was bipolar.

*

Hanging out with the boys was like being a teenager again. We played cards and chess, smoked outside and watched footy on the weekends. Eamon was popular and all his friends from private colleges turned up to meet him (Brad lived far away). Paul, a friend of mine, would come and visit me sometimes. I was very musically creative at the time and I would show Paul what I had done artistically.

*

When I finished my eleven days, all the usual things happened – I was picked up by my parents and I came home. But it was still apparent that I was elevated. So I went back to hospital for another seventeen days.

*

By the middle of June, I was well enough to leave. My dad drove me home and there was a sign on the door of my room saying 'Welcome Home'. I was still a touch high. This lasted about a week and then I was normal again. It took some getting used to.

*

In November, I went to my ten-year Radford Reunion. It was at the Youani Country Club. There were lawn bowls but I didn't bowl. I was funny and everything but I felt like I was somewhat of an outsider. Sometimes I felt comfortable in the company of others and other times bitterly alone. I left halfway through.

*

In December, I got a call from the ACT Writers Centre. They told me *Southbound* had been shortlisted for the 2006 ACT Writing and Publishing Award for Poetry. They wanted me to attend the Writers Centre Christmas Party. So I did and *Southbound* won the award. On the strength of this award, I was in Wikipedia. It felt good.

2007

In January, I went on community radio station 2XX to read poetry. I had been regularly interviewed on Bill Tully's show *Soundprint* since 1997. I read 'Vietnam', 'The Blind Man and his Dog' (an *A Man of Emails* outtake) and 'Love'.

*

In the late noughties, I went to the Front (a music and poetry venue) in Lyneham a number of times to read poetry at poetry slams. I read my poetry, I listened to people read, drank a bit and talked to some women. In April, I read two poems there – 'Study of a Wrecked Car' and 'Codral'. Here is 'Study of a Wrecked Car':

Study of a Wrecked Car

When I came back to my place,
on a bicycle, I noticed the wrecked car,
my face was plastered with sweat.
I have decided to come back to this wrecked car,
this smashed and burnt car, this derelict car.
After passing two giggling girls
and graffiti on some worn, pinkish-red planks,
I have come to this car, my arse on grass.
The whole thing went up in flames.
The whole ground around it is burnt.
There's shattered glass, some sticks are scattered
near the top of a red balloon. Weird.
As the wind cleanses my weathered face,

the trees nearby are all over the place.
A stout man comes along,
his dog has floppy ears.
We converse, he thinks
this event is tragic, and he leaves.
One of the back doors has had it -
the textures and colours are amazing -
the whole door could be a painting by Turner.
This surreal and unreal car, this trashed car.
Who did this and for what reason?
All I know is that it's here and I'm observing it.
A man on a bicycle passes me -
his shirt is swollen like a sail.
I look at other parts of this car,
this butter-coloured car, this smashed
and derelict car, so much like a scar.
The place where petrol was once pumped in
is open like a gaping mouth.
One of the front doors has a garish number -
one hundred and forty-five -
scrawled in yellow spray-paint.
The glazed hood of the wrecked car
is wonky as an oyster shell
and light-brown, while the thin bits of metal
inside the wrecked car
could be out of a Dali painting.
Nearby, a frail bit of plastic
dances in the wind.
My back is getting sore
and I know it's time to leave
this wrecked car, this burnt car,
this smashed and trashed car, this derelict car.

*

In 2007, I was trying to quit smoking. I had such a battle with it that my parents arranged for me to see a psychologist. She was good and I quit for a while. But I started again when I started working.

*

The day before I started work, I did my reading at the Gods café on the ANU campus. I made one mispronunciation. I read 'In the Near Future', 'Estuary at Dusk', 'At the Library', 'My First Lithium', 'The Similes and Metaphors Alone', 'The Hallowed House of Nevermind' (an *A Man of Emails* outtake), 'Shane Warne' (another *A Man of Emails* outtake), 'Retrospective' (from Serbian Literary Journal *Treci Trg*), 'Poem for Craig Nicholls', 'An Oppressive Summer Storm', 'The Death Knell', 'The Virus I Caught from the Television' and 'The Catwalk'. John Foulcher said my top three poems were 'My First Lithium', 'The Similes and Metaphors Alone' and 'The Virus I Caught from the Television'.

*

I met Ken Weaver (a salesman for *The Word*) on the day of the reading. I remember him being a scruffy guy and a smoker. He offered me one of his rollies and I accepted. We went into his house and we talked.

'Come back tomorrow and I'll show you what you need to know,' he said.

Before that, Workways (an organisation that helps people find work) had done some job searching for me re *The Word*. *The Word* were interested in me and impressed by my Masters in Journalism. I met John (the boss), who I won over by reciting 'Tuross, 1984'. I also told him I was bipolar but I had it under control.

*

The next day, I met Sylvia (Ken's wife). She offered me a Stuyvie, which I accepted, being my brand. Ken would write a spiel for me and I would read it out over the phone in my role as a salesman. In my first few days, I made a time to see the Scripture Union. That night, I practised my sales technique on Dad. I had a sheet that showed the cost of each ad and I went through it all. The next day I showed up at the Scripture Union's rooms. Before I went in, I smoked a cigarette for good luck. Then I went in and met the people and explained the different-sized ads and so forth. At the end, they bought a reasonable-sized ad in *The Word*.

I drove to the Weavers' place in the Inner North of Canberra. There was a fair bit of conversation going on in the house, then everyone looked at me.

'I sold my first ad,' I said.

Everyone came over and congratulated me.

*

The Weavers had two pet lorikeets – Rupert and Precious. They flew around the house. After work one day, I went outside – with Precious on my shoulder (I just thought she was tame). Precious flew off into a tree. I let the Weavers know and a number of us tried calling the bird down. Then a hose was used. As a result, the bird flew out of the tree and away. We looked for it that night. I came early the next morning to help the Weavers look for Precious. Then, about midday that day, a neighbour arrived with her. I was so relieved. If we had lost that lorikeet, it would have been the one regret I had in working for *The Word*. Fortunately, I have none.

*

I sold three ads for *The Word* and wrote two feature articles. I also helped with deliveries. In my last phase of working with *The Word*, I was instructed to undertake research incorporating logical progressions. The work was making me stressed. I was advised by my psychiatrist to quit. John offered me a role as a journalist for *The Word* but in the end I was too stressed out. In my email outlining my reasons for quitting, I also quoted Shakespeare: 'Parting is such sweet sorrow.'

*

In November, I spent eleven days in the psych ward 2N and in Hyson Green. I felt I wasn't getting anything done, I hadn't been sleeping and concentrating well and my thinking was askew.

*

In November, I went to a GLBTI night at Toast. I was keen to experiment with my sexuality. I talked to a gay guy for a while, then I went over to a very gay guy. I asked him, 'What do you think of bisexuals?'

He said, 'They're just straight guys that can't get girlfriends!'

I ended up chatting to these two young guys. I danced with them at one stage. I was perceived throughout the night as straight and I didn't do anything too gay. But I loved their company. Anyway, I went somewhere else, got a vodka cruiser, walked to the car park, couldn't find my car and decided to get a taxi home, all the time with a smile on my face.

*

After that night, I did some consideration of my sexuality. I was a little bit gay but mostly straight.

*

On the last day of December, I went bodyboarding for one last time at One-tree Beach in Tuross. It was a big day and I paddled out the back.

But ever since nearly drowning at Airport Beach, I hadn't been feeling comfortable in the water. Also, there was the matter of my vision: I couldn't see very well without my glasses. So I took a wave in. It was the end of an era. I had been a bodyboarder ever since I was fourteen and now I was twenty-nine. I just knew that was the end.

2008

In February, I tried to kill myself. In the process of trying, I had two beers and about fifty milligrams of Valium, which made me sick. So I went to the shops and bought a Sunkist and swallowed thirty sleeping pills. Dad found me pretty soon after taking the tablets. He had me count slowly to ten while he drove me to Calvary Hospital. They put me on a bed. I swallowed this black gunk which made me bring up all the tablets. I slept and when I woke next morning I promised Dad I would never try to kill myself again. He cried.

*

I would tell people I never considered myself to be a poet until I was published in *Quadrant*. Les Murray, the poetry editor of *Quadrant*, was like literary royalty to me. After ten years and about a dozen rejections, he finally published me. I had two poems, 'Heat' and 'My First Lithium', in the March issue of *Quadrant*. I also made the front cover (which listed some of the poets). It was amazing!

*

In April, for my thirtieth birthday, my mate Paul shouted me at the movies. We saw *U2 in 3D*. I loved it.

As we were walking back to my car, Paul said, 'They're pretty good for a three-piece.' This being muso talk, of course!

*

In June, I sent Geoff Page an email asking him about something I had floated with him earlier. At one of Geoff's book launches earlier in the year, I had discussed with him and Alan Gould the possibility of me doing an anthology of prose poems with Indigo (the Ginninderra Press imprint which Geoff and Alan Gould ran). Neither man was averse to the idea then. When I emailed them both about it mid-year, they were both encouraging. It was the start of the best job I've ever had.

*

In July, I emailed Stephen Matthews of Ginninderra Press about publishing a short, thermal-bound book, which I would call *A Man of Emails*. Within a day, he said he would do it.

*

In August, I gave my sixteen-poem *A Man of Emails* manuscript to poet and teacher John Foulcher to critique. I got it back soon after.

*

In August, I searched the poetry section of the ADFA Library. I was able to find plenty of good Australian prose poems.

*

In November, my maternal grandmother died. She was ninety-one. My family went down to Elmore, Victoria. We paid our last respects. I took heart in the fact that at her funeral I read a poem well about baking. The poem was called 'Cakes' and it was by Barbara Fisher. I read it because Nan was always baking.

*

In November, I saw (and heard) Lachlan Coventry's jazz band. It was the first time I had been exposed to jazz and I liked it. I gave a copy of *Southbound* to him. I wanted to give it to him for free but he insisted on paying for it. The next week, Lachlan phoned me up and we talked for about an hour. His favourite poem in *Southbound* was 'Memories of Wollongong' – a poem about surfing. 'Taking the lefts and smoking them,' I quoted to him.

2009

In 2009, I kept working on *The Indigo Book of Australian Prose Poems*. Early in 2009, I corresponded with notable Australian poet John Kinsella. I took two of his prose poems for the anthology.

*

In March, Geoff (one of my anthology bosses) told me the anthology was going ahead. He said there were still poems to be anthologised. Also, he told me the anthology must be in thematic order. That night, I came home and laid all the prose poems out on my living room rug. It took me a while, but I was able to arrange them into thematic order.

*

In April, I spent my thirty-first birthday having coffee with Bill Tully. We went to McCafé, which he patronises. We talked for an hour about literary figures we knew. Then Bill pulled up stumps and we headed to my car. We walked part of the way there and parted ways near a traffic island. I gave him the thumbs up.

*

In June, I found out I had a poem in *The Best Australian Poetry 2009*. Alan Wearne had taken 'Heat' from an edition of *Quadrant* in 2008. I found out via Martin Duwell, who elicited some notes and a bio from me.

I remember my mum telling someone on the phone with pride that I had a poem in the anthology.

I changed it before I put it in. John Foulcher helped me with the second last line. He didn't like 'As long as she is in it, and of it' in the *Quadrant* version.

'Got any ideas for that line?' I asked John.

'How about, "As long as she is burning in it"?' said John.

'Fantastic,' I said.

But the line became 'As long as she is burning within it.' I needed the extra syllable.

Heat

> You think I would be untrue,
> you think I would be a liar,
> if I were to say to you
> that your swimming pool is on fire.
> But it actually and factually is.
> In flames like a burning pyre,
> incandescent like a Roman candle,
> your swimming pool is on fire.
> For your beautiful daughter is bathing.
> Her breasts and legs I admire.
> As long as she is burning within it,
> your swimming pool is on fire!

'Heat' was part of my *A Man of Emails* manuscript which became a book in 2010.

*

During the middle of the year, I did a paid reading called Verse in the Vines at the Mount Majura Vineyard. I was on a quadruple bill with Elizabeth Lawson, Melinda Smith and S.K. Kelen. In my reading, I made one mispronunciation and read slowly. Some of the crowd were vocal. During 'Heat', they would say 'your swimming pool is on fire' every time I said it in the poem! At the end, Alan Gould congratulated me on the reading. I picked the right poems and I read them well.

*

In October, I did some work for the ACT Writers Centre. I was given the role of judge for the 2009 ACT Poets Lunch. I was paid with a free lunch on the day of the Poets Lunch and free wine with it.

*

In November, I received news that I had funding from artsACT for *The Indigo Book of Australian Prose Poems*. The grant was $5,827. This was a huge relief because otherwise I would have had to fund the project myself. I told Geoff and he loved it.

2010

Early in 2010, I drank Red Bulls for two weeks and paid for it with insomnia. My mood was also slightly elevated. I had three sleepless nights in a week and went to hospital. I wrote a poem about that experience called 'Insomnia' – my first substantial poem since 2006. Here it is:

Insomnia

Here I am, smoking a cigarette,
on a cool Thursday dawn
outside a hospital. I inhale acrid smoke.
The top lights up like a Christmas tree
but this January has not been festive.
Three sleepless nights in a week.
And now another. I stub my butt
among the mess that stressed people
have made. Some talk, here, outside.
Crickets compete with each other.
I go inside and chat with a male nurse
with a welcome sense of humour.
Then I go outside for another cigarette
smoked faster this time. Back inside,
I slouch in my chair, pacified and numbed
by the glossy infomercials making promises
not for me. Magazines slump on chairs.
I see a doctor – clinical, methodical,
thorough. Reluctant to give me Valium,
he's interested in a long term solution,
something that gets my sleeping back on track.

> We part. I feel content but as alert as ever.
> I find this place congenial but I know
> I should stay awake to the possibility of sleep.

*

In February, I went to a Les Murray reading at the Gods on the ANU campus. Before the reading started, I was looking for a seat. I was invited to sit opposite Les and Joyce Freedman (a poet).

'Yeah, I'll talk to Les and Joyce,' I said.

Les said, '"Heat", which he had published in *Quadrant*. I was coming up in the world. I was conversing with Les Murray – the best poet in Australia.

*

Les started by asking about my mental health. I told him I was a little elevated and he seemed to understand. Les, Joyce and I talked grouse, psychiatrists, golf, performing, getting published and other matters. At the end of the evening, Les had left his hat where I was sitting. I picked it up and gave it to him. He was most grateful.

'May you never be pronounced hatless,' I said.

*

Later in February, I managed eleven hours sleep for the first time in ages. I saw my psychiatrist. He said to steer clear of energy drinks. He also said I was completely normal.

*

In late April, I had a launch of *A Man of Emails*. I met Marc there and we swapped contact details. Bill Tully launched the book and he did a good job. Among those who attended were my Uncle Garry, Dad's friend Wally and Alan Gould, John Foulcher and Penelope Cottier. I gave a speech and read some poems. I only made one mispronunciation reading the poems – at the end of the third (and final) poem. Then Bill had dinner with my family. A good night was had by all.

*

All through 2010, I was working on *The Indigo Book of Australian Prose Poems*. I had sent a routine email to Geoff Page in October stating the launch of the anthology could be early in December. Geoff responded by saying Stephen Matthews (my publisher) had had health problems in the last month or two.

*

By late October, I knew what was wrong. Stephen was at home after two weeks in hospital and facing six weeks of radiotherapy.

*

By early November, it was sorted. I had spoken to Geoff and we had come to the conclusion that if Stephen couldn't do it, we couldn't do it. Geoff had suggested mid-February.

'Many, many thanks. Mid-February should present no problems,' said Stephen in an email.

2011

In late February, I had a poem accepted for publication. *The Canberra Times* took 'Lake Ginninderra', which was an old poem that featured in *Southbound*.

*

On Friday 25 March, *The Indigo Book of Australian Prose Poems* was launched by Adrian Caesar at Dalton's Bookshop in Canberra. There was a sizeable crowd and about thirty books were sold. Adrian made a speech, then I made a speech. Then I introduced John Foulcher, Geoff Page, Alan Gould and P.S. Cottier, who all read their prose poems. After that, I read a prose poem. All four had read flawlessly and I felt some pressure to read well. Fortunately, I read without any mispronunciations. Then my family had dinner at Tosolini's (a Canberra restaurant) with some of the contributors. I remember arriving home and going for a walk. It was a nice night and I remember looking up at the stars and just feeling wonderful.

*

Soon after, Geoff said in an email that he wanted to meet up with me at Providore (a Canberra café) once I sent off the books and cheques to contributors. He said he would shout me a well-deserved cappuccino.

*

In early April, I received an email from John Kinsella (one of Australia's best poets). He had two prose poems in the anthology. Anyway, the email was praising of *The Indigo Book of Australian Prose Poems*. He said the anthology was 'superb'. He said he admired my 'work' and 'scope of editorial vision'. He said I hadn't just played it safe – I had a genuine range of 'voices'.

*

After things had settled down with *The Indigo Book of Australian Prose Poems*, I began working on a review I would pitch to *The Canberra Times*. I was an apprentice reviewer. Geoff gave me a book called *This Floating World* by Libby Hart to read and offered to help me out with it. It went through numerous drafts, with Geoff making some corrections. Finally, it was accepted by *The Canberra Times* and published on Saturday, 3 September 2011 (see Articles and Reviews).

*

During the middle of the year, I helped a young man from Queanbeyan with his poetry. I was paid to assess his manuscript and he also paid for a thirty-minute consultation. I talked to him about his poetry – what his strengths and weaknesses were, writing a mature poem and the classless nature of poetry. At the end of the consultation, I gave him *The Song in Your Head* (a poetry textbook for secondary school students) by John Foulcher and a copy of *Southbound*. I told him to read, read, read.

*

Also, during the middle of the year, I was accepted into a poetry anthology team, working for Australian Poetry. There were about a dozen of us and we were to put together a members' anthology. We were to communicate via Facebook. I wasn't on Facebook at the time. My sister helped me with getting on it. Anyway, I dropped out of the team because I was having mental health issues. But I remained on Facebook. One of my earliest posts was, 'I'm more of a poet than anything else.'

*

After my first review was published, I began on a second review for *The Canberra Times*. Geoff gave me *Surface to Air* by Jaya Savige and again offered to help me with the review. I read the book twice. It was a pleasure to read, just like *This Floating World*. The review was published on Saturday, 19 November 2011 (see Articles and Reviews).

*

In December, I received an email from the ACT Writers Centre to come along to their Christmas party. I'd been notified about coming along to this event previously in 2006 and I went on to win the 2006 ACT Writing and Publishing Award for Poetry. But I didn't take it for granted that I had won this time round. You never know. Anyway, I did win the 2011 ACT Writing and Publishing Award for Poetry. It was for my third book of poetry titled *A Man of Emails*. It was four years in the making and had taken a few twists and turns.

2012

Early in 2012, I started playing Scrabble on Wednesdays at the Southern Cross Club in Woden. I wanted to see how good I was after beating Mum a lot of the time in domestic games. Against tournament players, I won one game out of twelve and nearly won another two. I loved those nights but after a while I felt more comfortable playing Mum with all the things I had learnt from the tournament players.

*

In March, I had a review published in *The Canberra Times*. When it was sent by email to Gia Metherell (the paper's literary editor), she found a couple of sentences that didn't make sense. She fixed them and ran the review in *The Canberra Times* on Saturday 3 March 2012 (see Articles and Reviews). But she told Geoff, who told me, that I was no longer needed as a reviewer for *The Canberra Times*. It was unfortunate. I was having addiction issues at the time with energy drinks. I eventually kicked them.

*

In July, I had a poetry reading at the Gods. I was on a triple bill with Suzanne Edgar and Paul Magee. I cleared my head of energy drinks and alcohol beforehand (although I had a beer after). I read reasonably well, making three mispronunciations (two in 'Waiting for the Mail' and one in 'Airport Beach in Summer'). I allow myself three at the most. Fortunately, I nailed the last four poems. In addition to 'Waiting for the Mail' and 'Airport Beach in Summer', I read 'Photograph of Two Friends', 'The Voices', 'Mania', 'Words', 'Heat', 'My First Lithium', 'The Virus I

Caught from the Television' and 'The Catwalk'. Then, at the end of the night I was asked to read 'The Death Knell' and 'Theatre'. I sold a *Southbound* for twenty dollars and *A Man of Emails* for fifteen dollars.

*

Soon after, Steve Kelen phoned me up. He said, 'I heard you did a good reading.' Steve has always been encouraging of my poetic efforts. It was a nice gesture.

*

After my setback with reviewing for *The Canberra Times*, I decided I still wanted to be a poetry reviewer. In 2012, I was reviewing Ginninderra Press titles for *eVoice* (part of the Ginninderra Press website). Stephen Matthews, who put up each review, was encouraging of my efforts.

*

In October, I was having coffee with Bill when he told me about an idea he had. It involved poets reading on the 'soapbox' in front of the busts of three poets at Garema Place in Civic, Canberra. The three busts were of Judith Wright, A.D. Hope and David Campbell. Anyway, I thought it was a good idea. We both turned up at 10.30 on a Thursday. We both said some stuff and read a few poems.

As I was walking back to my car with Bill, I asked him what he wanted to call this venture.

'Poet's Point,' he said.

*

In December, I received the 2012 ACT Writing and Publishing Award for Poetry for *The Indigo Book of Australian Prose Poems*. I put a lot of hard work into it. It was good that I was rewarded for my efforts in that way. I posted the news on Facebook and had a number of likes.

*

The Indigo Book of Australian Prose Poems is now featured in ten libraries around Australia. These are Deakin University Library, Libraries ACT, Monash University Library, National Library of Australia, State Library of NSW, State Library of South Australia, State Library of Western Australia, The University of Melbourne Library, University of Queensland Library and University of Western Australia Library.

2013

In February, I bought (with the help of my parents) a town house in Holt for me to live in. There were a few things to fix outside the house but the house itself was fully renovated and close to Kippax shops and a few ovals.

*

In March, I went fundraising for Red Cross. One woman down my street gave me twenty dollars. One woman flirted with me and a woman who used to collect for Red Cross bonded with me. I collected sixty-seven dollars.

*

In April, I visited Marc (a mate) in hospital three times. The first time, we played Scrabble and Marc won. The second time, we played a game of chess and he won. Then the last time, we played a game of Scrabble and I won. Marc is also a poet and we wrote a poem together. Marc's contributions are in italics.

Anarchy in the ACT

Flustered, anarchic *tendencies draw us*
as we walk through Garema Place
whose inhabitants sprawl
as Bill lights up Poets Point.
Judith Wright's stern visage
surveys the scene, *and I'm shouting to be heard.*

Michael Byrne steps up
and the pigeons are startled.
Cute girls in short shorts *walk by gaily,*
overhearing, overheating, digging hands in backs.
Chess becomes the sky
clouds to fuck knows what!
Is there a sense of the oppressed,
Are we watched at all?
As the poets rise to the call…

Early in June, I did a paid reading at Manning Clark House in Canberra. I was on a triple bill with Alan Gould and Jessica Wilkinson. I had just been out at a restaurant with my parents and Bill. Bill is my lucky charm; whenever I go somewhere with him I usually have good fortune. I read twelve poems from *A Man of Emails* – 'Heat', 'My First Lithium', 'The Similes and Metaphors Alone', 'Life with Your Very First Set of Wheels', 'Sunday', 'Poem for Craig Nicholls', 'Love', 'Vietnam', 'An Oppressive Summer Storm', 'The Cockatoo', 'The Virus I Caught from the Television' and 'The Catwalk'. Anyway, I made no mispronunciations. It was the best reading I had ever done.

*

Late in June, I went into my new place. For the first few days, I was on a high. I posted something on Facebook – a parody of 'A Sort of Homecoming' by U2 called 'A Sort of Housewarming'. It went, 'and you know it's time to go / to this townhouse that you know…'

*

In mid-July I attended the Turner exhibition at the National Gallery. I was taken aback by a painting called *The Tenth Plague of Egypt*. I borrowed a pen from my sister and wrote a few lines on a ticket. I also bought a book about Turner which had a picture of the painting in it.

So I began work on it – drafting and drafting. I showed it to Geoff, who suggested I make it longer, which was a good idea.

Eventually it was finished and now 'The Tenth Plague of Egypt by Turner' is one of my best new poems.

*

In August, I found out I had a poem, 'In the Near Future', in *The Stars Like Sand: Australian Speculative Poetry* edited by Tim Jones and P.S. Cottier. I wrote 'In the Near Future' when I was seventeen. It was exciting to get it anthologised. Here is the poem:

In the Near Future

Optic fibres
are the veins of this city,
wrapping through the backyards
of the new suburbs, extending
towards the horizon. The sky accepts
the meagre process
of matchbox cars cluttering a freeway,
a hockey match, fought on astroturf,
new housing estates clinging
to the outskirts…
Yet the sky demands less of it,
water gathered
in a grey vortex of cloud.
The air grows cold.
And hailstones
pelt the concrete.

*

In December, my *New and Selected Poems* was accepted for publication by Ginninderra Press. My *New and Selected Poems* contained six poems from *Estuary at Dusk* as well as twenty poems and eight poems from *Southbound* and *A Man of Emails* respectively. There were also six new poems.

*

In December, I went to visit my sister Jen and her partner Jane at their place at Thirroul, Wollongong. I participated in the Pinky Cup (a table tennis tournament involving the four members of my family and Jane). I came third out of five people – Jen first, then Dad, then me, then Jane, then Mum.

*

At the end of December, I went down the coast. Adam Hills (host of the TV shows *Spicks and Specks* as well as *The Last Leg*) was staying at Tuross also. Adam is the grandson of Chris Hills, who lived next door to our place down the coast. I gave him a copy of *A Man of Emails*. A few years previous to that, I gave him a copy of *Southbound* and he gave me some positive feedback on it. He's a nice guy.

2014

In March, after a month of laboured breathing and lack of sleep, I was diagnosed with sinusitis by my doctor. My doctor said use a nasal spray. She also proscribed some antibiotics. After being diagnosed and treated, I gradually became better.

*

In March, I read a poem, 'Do Not Stand at My Grave and Weep', at my paternal grandmother's funeral. She requested I read the poem. She lived until she was ninety-eight and died peacefully. My grandmother was an amazing woman. I remember telling her (the last time I saw her) that she had made it to 2014. She looked at me with wonder. Nan had the idea that I was a poet before I did. She always took an interest in my poetry and literature generally. She was beautiful.

*

In late April, one of Australia's best young poets, Robbie Coburn, introduced himself to me by wishing me a belated happy birthday on Facebook. I've gone on to like some of his posts, and he has liked some of mine.

*

In May, I helped a friend (Geoff Campbell) out with his poetry. Geoff is a mathematician and an ex-AFL umpire. We met up at a café and talked for a while. Then he sent me some poems which I critiqued. He thanked me for my constructive criticism.

*

In July, I received the proofs for my *New and Selected Poems*. They were okay but I felt six changes ought to be made. I emailed the changes to Stephen Matthews and he said they were sensible enough.

*

In late October, I had the launch of my *New and Selected Poems*. I had an injection for my mental health the day before and I felt really good. On that day, I was switched on. Bill Tully, who launched the book, was too. I didn't make any mistakes in my speech or the reading of the poems.

*

In December, I posted on Facebook, 'I have a plan. To get my best comedy sketches performed on stage.'

2015

In March, I posted some footage on Facebook of Carlton player Lance Whitnall kicking a goal against Essendon late in the 1999 preliminary final. If Lance hadn't kicked it, we wouldn't have won. That game converted me to Carlton after being a Swans supporter for a number of years. I still barrack for Carlton through the bad times and the good.

*

In March, I went to the launch of a Canberra poetry anthology – *The House is Not Quiet and The World is Not Calm* edited by Kit Kelen and Geoff Page. I had four poems in it – 'Mania', 'The Virus I Caught from the Television', 'Theatre' and 'Heat'. Each poet was to read and I read 'Heat' well.

*

In March, after stating on Facebook that I wanted to get my best comedy sketches performed on stage, I emailed an ex-teacher of mine and thespian, George Huitker. I pointed out that I had helped him get his poetry and prose poetry published. Now I was asking him for a favour. Could he help me with getting my comedy sketches on stage? He let me know of a couple of people in the area. Then he abandoned the project but said he would come back to it 'sometime'.

*

In April, I announced on Facebook that I had decided to play table tennis competitively in Canberra. I had got a table tennis bat for my birthday. I had also decided to become a member of TTACT (Table Tennis ACT). I looked forward to whacking some balls.

*

In late May, I picked up my new car (a Renault Clio) from Rolfe Motors in Belconnen. I had crashed my previous car (a Nissan Pulsar SLX) in wet conditions going around a corner into my street. It was a write-off. Having a new car represented a new level of freedom for me. I wasn't asking Dad to drive me around in his car. Dad drove the car to Hall (an out-of-the-way suburb of Canberra) so I could practise driving my new car for the first time.

*

In June, I joined TTACT. Once I had filled out my form and sent the cheque, the emails started coming in. My first one was from Song Chen – centre manager with TTACT. This was good.

*

In June, I encountered Lachlan Coventry at the Florey shops. We talked while his daughter played on some play equipment. I pointed out my car and told him I was happy with it. 'It's got the soul of a sports car,' I said.

*

In July, I formally interviewed Geoff Page. I had done a lot of preparation and had decided on a Q and A format. The interview was to be published on my website (https://poetrybymichaelbyrne.wordpress.com). Geoff would have a look at it first, though. It went really well. Geoff said some good stuff. Coming home, I listened to the interview. There was the rush you get from doing journalism that I hadn't felt since my Masters. I'm not ruling out interviewing more poets.

*

In August, I played table tennis in Kingston. We started in the morning and I hadn't quite woken up. I remember playing nine games of doubles and winning two. This was okay considering I hadn't played much doubles before. It lasted three hours and it was ongoing playing. I had trouble concentrating for that long. But it was okay and the people were nice. But I knew I wasn't coming back next week.

*

In September, I had lunch at Grazing (Gundaroo) with Mum, Dad, my sister and her partner Jane. I don't say much in group conversations. However, I've had lunch with these people a number of times and I still enjoy it.

*

In October, I went to the Stencil Art Prize launch in Sydney. My sister had some stencil art being displayed and was shortlisted for the prize. At the end of the night, the awards were announced. My sister didn't win anything.

I turned around to her. 'You're still really good,' I said.

She laughed.

*

In December, Dad and I went to the ACT Writers Centre Christmas Party. The ACT Writing and Publishing Awards for 2015 were being announced. I had entered my *New and Selected Poems* in the Poetry award. I knew I hadn't won it, though – I hadn't been asked to attend. But I was curious to find out who had won the Poetry award. P.S. Cottier came second with *The Stars Like Sand* – it was a good anthology and it deserved an award. John Stokes came first. He's a good poet.

2016

In late January, I booked two seats for my mother and me to attend a Les Murray reading. It was on the ANU campus on 9 February. Before that, at Christmas, I had been given two books of poetry authored by Les Murray – *Waiting for the Past* and *On Bunyah*. Anyway, preceding the Murray reading, I read *Waiting for the Past* three times. In the first half of the reading, Murray read from *Waiting for the Past* and I took most of it in. Then, in the second half, he read from *On Bunyah* (which I hadn't read). I was inattentive in the second half. So it was a tale of two halves.

*

In late February, I had coffee at Urban Pantry with Geoff Page. I had gotten to know him a bit better with my work on *The Indigo Book of Australian Prose Poems*. Geoff is funny, a really good poet, and he has helped me with reviews and getting readings in the past. A nice guy.

*

In early March, I went with Dad to the Scarfe Room on the ANU campus to hear Kathleen Bleakley, John Foulcher and Suzanne Edgar read. All three are good poets but not difficult poets. I was attentive for the full reading.

*

In early April, I went to the Petra White/Iggy McGovern reading. I had done my homework with White. She read some new stuff but most of the stuff she read I had read before. I paid attention. It was interesting to encounter her in person, as I had previously only known her from Facebook. Anyway, Iggy McGovern was a difficult poet. I wasn't very attentive with him. So a tale of two halves again.

*

In early July, Mum forwarded an email from Denise Burton. She was an anthologist, inviting me to submit up to two poems to be included in a chapbook being launched and performed during Mental Health Week 2016. I decided to send her a couple of poems. Eventually I settled on 'Mania' and 'The Voices'. They were two of my best poems about mental illness. Here is 'Mania':

Mania

Mania precluded and included university.
Mania was being massaged to sleep.
Mania was soothing fingers
on my skin, and fists beating
on my back, drumming out demons.
Mania was being reassured,
mania was pacing my room, my house,
Canberra. Mania brought white blisters.
Mania was restless hyperactivity
and persistent hunger. Mania was hell.
Mania was refusing to sleep, and hiding
beer in my room. Dad found it anyway.
Mania was being paranoid as Stalin.
Mania was fighting with my parents,
slamming an iron fist down on the table.
Mania brought a cackle from a jackal –
spontaneous, it came for no reason,
the same animal was brought
to the calm waiting room of a psychiatrist,

staring blankly, looking frightened.
Mania was nearly punching my dad,
holding back my fist like a hammer.
Mania was being up and down,
euphoria and serving a sentence,
my moods swinging
like endless night into glaring day.
Mania was cured by Zyprexa.
Mania broke down like a pill
in my body. I was content to live.
And now, I've woken up to sleep.

*

On the first day of spring, my sister gave birth. It was a boy and his name was Avery. Soon after, my parents and I visited my sister and her partner and Avery in hospital. I had an opportunity to hold the baby. I had never held a baby before. The first couple of times, he was as good as gold.

I said, 'I'm winning by doing nothing.'

Then he cried on me. Such is life. Also, I'm now an uncle. I'm looking forward to reading children's books to him.

*

In early September, I phoned Bill Tully after eighteen months. I wasn't sure how he would react but he was down with it. We talked for about forty minutes. He was funny at times and so was I. Then on a Thursday we had Poet's Point but it was raining, so we went to Donut King. I had a Coke and he had a flat white (very hot). We had a really good conversation.

*

In October, Bill didn't show up to Poet's Point one week. So Mark Scully and I went to a café and read each other poems for about half an hour. Then neither man turned up the week after, so I drove home. I realised that Bill was getting too old to be regimented to come to Poet's Point. I brought that up with Bill in a phone conversation. We were sick of each other by then too, so we agreed to give each other some space. So that was the resurrection of Poet's Point – one week with me and Bill and Mark Scully before Bill started not to show.

*

On Sunday, 9 October, I went to *Beatles in Symphony* in Llewellyn Hall with Dad. The orchestra, conducted by Guy Noble, played Beatles songs. I knew all the songs and had a thoroughly good time. They had audience participation at the end and I sang a bit (but Dad didn't). The conductor was really funny. I also liked looking at one of the musicians, who was enjoying herself while playing.

*

On Monday, 10 October at 5 p.m. at Smiths Alternative Bookshop, I attended the launch of *The Lived Experience* – an anthology of Mental Health Consumers in the ACT. I liked the diversity of voices on the night. I read 'The Voices' (my first poem) well. I had rehearsed it and it was fine. Then later on in the evening, Laurie (Denise's partner) called on readers to use up some time. I was asked to read 'Mania'. As a favour to Laurie, I read it. Normally, I rehearse poems I read in public but I thought reading 'Mania' would be okay. I made one mispronunciation in the middle of the poem and two at the end. I walked off the stage pissed off. My only solace was that I read the first poem well.

*

Also on 10 October, I received an email from Geoff about a CD that featured him and some jazz musicians collaborating in 2015 at the Bungendore Wood Works café. One of the jazz musicians (the guitarist) was Lachlan Coventry – a mate of mine who I see from time to time. It sounded really good. I gave my postal address to Geoff and he put the CD in the post the next day. When I listened to the fusion of jazz and poetry, it was wonderful.

*

In Mid-December, my sister sent me an email with footage of singer Patti Smith. She was singing a Bob Dylan song at the 2016 Nobel Prize ceremony. She forgot the lyrics to the song a couple of times. I admired her composure when she first forgot the lyrics: she simply said she was nervous and the audience understood. After viewing her rendition of the song, I read an article by Patti Smith. My sister sent it to me. Patti Smith put the performance into perspective. She did it well. I could identify with Patti Smith with my three mispronunciations during my reading of 'Mania' at the launch of *The Lived Experience*.

2017–April 2018

At the start of 2017, I was well into hearing hallucinatory voices for my schizophrenia. I would nominate someone in my head. The voice that was always there would read my thoughts and let me know whether I could talk to the guest voice. Sometimes the person had a silent number. Sometimes the person would say they didn't want to do it, but he or she would say I was 'okay'. But sometimes I could talk to the guest voice. The voice that was always there would take charge. I might contribute to the voices every now and again. Sometimes I would insult the guest voices then apologise profusely. The stress of insulting pretty much stopped when I was put on Clozapine.

*

In July, I started on Clozapine (for my schizophrenia). I started on half a tablet. Then, in a measured way, the dosage was increased. I was staying at my parent's house and on weeknights I would watch *Letters and Numbers*. Lily Serna, the maths whiz on the show, was told by contestants which various mathematical combinations to use (two large, four small et cetera). Anyway, at night I would call out my dosage of Clozapine (two large, two small et cetera) to my parents. I had to make sure.

*

In mid-October, I had a poem 'Marijuana Days' in a play called *Under Sedation* held in the Street Theatre, Canberra. When I was hearing my prose poem recited, I was amazed how much the actor (Ben Drysdale) could recall of the (long) prose poem. Anyway, here is the poem:

Marijuana Days

We would cruise into Civic, ogle anything that moved, then Craig would saunter into a flat or whatever and score a stick while I would stare at some tazos. Those harmless holograms were a preview of what was to come, for me anyway. We would drive to the top of a mountain – once, in his eagerness to get bent, Craig got a speeding fine – I'm sure he clocked one-fifty.

The second time we got stoned he kept on prodding me – as if an eyebrow that was cut, lit and tapped out of a small metal cone could evince his true personality. At the pinnacle of the high, he would almost always play *The Prodigy* – every time I hear 'Breathe' I can recall it all. And once after some 'buds' or 'skunk', he wisely asked me if I wanted to sniff petrol. He did worse things to me – while I was perched up a tree he poured bong water over my head, my hemp shirt reeking of pot. Then he prodded me again, this time with his foot as I laid on his backyard lawn – seeing all the colours of the rainbow and then some. His home produce was lethal.

And once I met his supplier in his natural habit. Dressed in a poncho, a superior bong in his hand, he reminded me more of the caterpillar from *Alice in Wonderland* than a human being. Then Craig raced down the stairs and I followed the best I could, curious about what would eventuate. We got to the car park. He made his car impenetrable, then opened a window and kindly spat on my sunglasses, leaving me to walk from Civic to Belconnen. I cursed him all the way home.

Why did I smoke pot with Craig a dozen times? It wasn't for the farcical moments – him getting a plastic bottle from a rubbish bin, me walking into his garage, me reciting T.S. Eliot's 'Preludes' in his presence.

It wasn't for his company. It was more to inspire poetry – and it did. It's just a shame that the great depression followed this. My psychiatrist found out about Craig and instantly hated him, my parents banished me from seeing him and I grew to loathe him. I walked down a path, realised it was not for me and walked back through gloomy weather clouding my neurochemistry.

In conclusion, some friend dead – end. The joke's on him – I'm still alive. The rest is history. Thank God he could drive.

*

In November, I went to see *Loving Vincent* – a movie about Vincent Van Gogh – with my mum. Before I saw it, I read up on it. There were numerous animators for it. That's what I remember about it – it was a lovely spectacle.

*

In November, my sister let me know about a message on my website. It read,

Hi Michael,

I am looking for some advice and editing help with my poetry. I have taken early retirement (age 56) and for the last 5 years have been painting and writing poetry in concert with the visual work. I have had a number of well received exhibitions where I have included some of my poetry. I am aiming now for the M16 Gallery in Canberra and need some professional input as to the selection and fine tuning of the poems and the curatorial scope. Would you be interested?

Cheers, Lyza, Pambula Beach, NSW.

I took her up.

*

In early April, I sent an email to Marc. In the body of the email I sent was a poem I had just written. Marc loved it. Here it is:

Ode to my dad

Here is my dad in our backyard.
He is now in his seventies.
The lawnmower groans and drones.
I look down and see a lifetime:
Vietnam, marriage to my lovely mum,
public service and parenthood,
epilepsy, cancers cut out, rugby league,
landscaping, tennis, fixing things.
He says poetry is like a sport.

*

On 21 April, my family went to the MCG to watch an AFL match between Carlton and the West Coast Eagles. Apart from me (who barracks for the Blues), there was my dad (who barracks for the Swans), Mum (who barracks for Geelong), my cousin Greg (who barracks for Essendon), and my sister (nada team). Whether they barracked for a team or not, it was a nice gesture for members of my family to come along to help celebrate my fortieth birthday, even if it was a week early. Once the game started, Greg would make conversation with me and later he got me a lemonade. I don't remember too much about the game apart from the gulls and the smog and the fact that we lost but not badly. I think there were a couple of goals in it. We gave them a fright. West Coast ended up winning the flag. I also tramped some of Melbourne on my holiday. Or Marvellous Melbourne, as Les Murray called it.

My Poetry

Dad says it's like a sport and I agree with him. Reading is a bit like a contact sport – you need balls to do it. And the competitive nature of sending poems to journals – you lose or you win.

But most of all it's an art form. I mucked around at school doing visual art and drama. I was too repressed for acting but I was good at visual art. But I was better at poetry. I won a competition in year 12. It was like I'm actually good at something. I knew what I was going to do – be the best poet I could be.

I remember giving some poems to Geoff Page. He said I should send 'Heat', 'My First Lithium' and 'Life with Your Very First Set of Wheels' to *Quadrant*; they were the best of them. I did but I didn't think too much about it. I waited. Then, one day I was hanging around the house with my parents. I picked up an envelope from *Quadrant* and opened it. My parents crowded around me.

'I've got two poems published in *Quadrant*!' I said. It was good. Les Murray sent me a little note:

I've taken Heat and the masterly My First Lithium for Qdt. Cheers,
 – Les

And the poem that didn't make it? 'Life with Your Very First Set of Wheels' resides these days in my third book of poems, *A Man of Emails*.

What was really cool, apart from having Les Murray's approval and being in Australia's premier literary journal was that I was still in my twenties when the poems were published – just. It was March 2008, I was twenty-nine and had my birthday the next month. Anyway, my name was mentioned on the front cover of *Quadrant*. I had my two poems on page 51 – alongside a poem by Barbara Fisher and a hilarious spoof about a country diner.

In the next year, I was contacted by Martin Duwell, who told me that I had a poem in *The Best Australian Poetry 2009* (UQP). Alan Wearne had taken 'Heat' from *Quadrant* in the previous year. I was given the option of changing the poem. As mentioned earlier, John Foulcher didn't like the penultimate line, and I changed it. I also wanted to change the line 'In flames like a burning tyre' to 'In flames like a burning pyre'. It was more evocative.

I was also asked to write a bit about the poem, I proffered the following:

> Byrne writes of 'Heat': Everyone I know who has read 'Heat' says it's funny or it's clever how it resolves itself but I like the musicality of it. It has some qualities of a punk rock song.

Regular Reading Gigs

Soundprint

From 1997 to 2011, I participated on *Soundprint*, a Canberra radio show hosted by Bill Tully. I remember going on the show in 2008 after I had just been published in *Quadrant*. I was on a roll. I read 'My First Lithium', 'Heat' and 'Life with Your Very First Set of Wheels.' In my introduction to 'Heat', I said, 'This poem documents my work as a voyeurologist.'

Jamantics

In March 2006 I saw an ad for Jamantics at the Lighthouse in Belconnen in the ACT Writers Centre newsletter. This was of interest to me and a few other poets who turned up on the night. They did not show up next time. I stayed. Jim, the convenor, would allow me one poem between musician sets. I would hold up a finger and mouth 'one' to him and he would nod. People would talk and I would say, 'I want a calm blue ocean for the lighthouse!' I would read different poems but the two crowd favourites were 'Heat' and the notorious and previously unpublished 'Codeine'. Sometimes Jim, a guitarist, would perform with me. I remember performing my prose poem 'Marijuana Days' with Jim, who made trippy sounds on the guitar. I gave him a high five at the end. Early on, I was manic and I had the time of my life drinking and smoking and socialising and listening to musicians. Then I went into hospital and I would walk from Hyson Green to the Lighthouse at night. But soon I would come down and I wasn't enjoying myself as much. By December, my Lighthouse nights were over.

Poet's Point

In October 2012, I was sitting in a civic café with Bill Tully. He had an idea for a reading venture. He wanted me to turn up at 10.30 on Thursday at Garema Place near the statues of poets. I did and so did Bill. We read a few poems each, then decided to go. When I got to my car, Bill hugged me. Then I asked him what he wanted to call this venture. 'Poet's Point,' said Bill.

Bill became the host of Poet's Point and would read some poems. So did I. Bill would ask people going past to read a poem. Sometimes a poet would be discovered. Jim, one of the men who frequented Garema Place, recited some of his own bush verse. Bill and I were impressed with his yarns. Jim read a number of times at Poet's Point. Di, a woman, read poetic passages from the Bible a number of times at Poet's Point. One of Bill's friends, Tony, read his witty verse at Poet's Point – although curiously Di would not show when he was there. Tony had some relationship history with Di – Tony wasn't a fly repellent he was a Di repellent! Later, Mark Scully became the third poet at Poet's Point. Tully and Scully did not get along. There were also cracks appearing in my relationship with Bill. In early 2015, Poet's Point folded. In 2016, one Poet's Point with Tully, Scully and Byrne took place. But it couldn't be carried on due to discipline issues among poets.

My Books

Collections

Estuary at Dusk: Poems 1995–2000
This book was published by Stephen Matthews of Ginninderra Press (as with the rest of these books). The book has fifty-two poems. 'Estuary at Dusk' was the best poem (hence the title). When I was writing them, I wasn't thinking about literary fame or my reputation. It was great to be published and at a reasonably young age. I was twenty-three.

Southbound (Winner of the ACT Writing and Publishing Award for Poetry 2006)
I once referred to *Southbound* as Sourbound because it's such a bleak book! It preserved some intense emotional experiences, including the only poem I have written about schizophrenia ('The Voices'). The title refers to my love of the south coast of NSW. With this one, I obsessed over the manuscript. The book has forty poems. I worked hard on them. I wanted to have a book that was better than my first. I think I achieved my aim.

A Man of Emails (Winner of the ACT Writing and Publishing Award for Poetry 2011)
With this one I obsessed over the manuscript as well. The manuscript, in its original form, was sent back by Ginninderra Press. I culled it quite a bit and sent it to Geoff Page and then John Foulcher. Stephen eventually offered me a thermal-bound book with this one. I thought about it for a while, then said yes. I've had some good feedback for *A Man of Emails*. I received two good reviews for it. Also, local poets have said it's good.

New and Selected Poems
I think this book is as good as *A Man of Emails*. Out of the one hundred and twenty poems I've published, it brings together forty of my best ones. It also has 'Theatre' (a new poem) which was published in *Quadrant*. The new poem 'Insomnia' is about being manic (or up) and the new poem 'The Death Knell' is about depression. The first section begins with 'Volutions' – a poem I wrote in Year 11. It's about me feeling suicidal at school.

Anthologies

On Common Water
Anyone who has worked as an anthologist will tell you it's the most pleasant work. Namely, you get to express yourself through the poems you choose. Which is what I did with *On Common Water*. It was an in-house Ginninderra anthology so it wasn't too demanding. Stephen helped me out with it, as did my dad. One of the poems in the anthology, 'Dog', was penned by Leon Trainor. He said the five-dollar fee would go towards a cappuccino for himself and a pork sausage for his dog!

The Indigo Book of Australian Prose Poems (Winner of the ACT Writing and Publishing Award for Poetry 2012)
Early in 2008, I went to one of Geoff Page's book launches. There, with Geoff Page and Alan Gould (the men in charge of Ginninderra Press's poetry imprint Indigo), I floated the idea of an anthology of prose poems. They were agreeable. But I didn't think much more about it until midway through 2008. Then I floated the idea via email to Geoff and Alan again. They were encouraging. They said if I could get a decent manuscript together they would consider it. I went to the PR section of the ADFA Library, where I spent some time choosing prose poems. I ended up with 158, which got culled to 100 by Geoff and Alan. I had a manuscript. From there on, a few cards fell my way that would make the anthology a success. First of all, Indigo were publishing one more

book, which became *The Indigo Book of Australian Prose Poems*. Also, Geoff had retired from work and was able to liaise with me. Also, I applied for an artsACT grant to pay the poets. I got it. Also, Stephen got sick. But he recovered. After almost three years, *The Indigo Book of Australian Prose Poems* was launched.

Epilogue

My process in writing poetry was different in the early days than from now. In the early days, I was at my most prolific. Also, I just wanted to get published. I didn't think too much about it all. These days, I'm not as prolific. Also, I haven't sent out poems for a long time. I have had success with being included in anthologies, though.

What inspires me? Normally my poems are about the world and my place in it. There are a couple of poems which are conceptualised. Also, I wrote an ekphrastic poem (a poem about visual art) a few years ago.

I'm bipolar (I have sustained periods of mood swing). Sometimes, I write poetry when I'm a little high. 'Insomnia' is one such poem. Sometimes, I write poems about depression, such as 'Drowning'. I'm also schizophrenic. However, I've only ever written one poem about it 'The Voices'.

I cut my teeth on the Canberra poetry scene of the 1990s. I was torn between the Canberra performance scene and the literary one where the most important thing is what's on the page rather than on the stage. As I started to get more paid readings, I decided that what was on the page was the most important thing.

I've only really had two mentors. John Foulcher was my first. He would tick my poems, cross out lines and use words to convey things in my poems. I remember him helping me with the ending of a poem. Geoff Page is my current mentor. He's a stickler for rhyme and metre. He was also my boss for *The Indigo Book of Australian Prose Poems*.

I'm not as creative as I used to be. Since 2006, I was put on Lithium again, which stymied my creativity. Since then, I've written one or two poems in a year. Sometimes, in a year, I might write nothing. In 2018,

I wrote three poems. The three were all written under the influence of Clozapine. I started on it in the middle of 2017. Since then, the hallucinatory voices have been less intrusive.

Articles and Reviews

From 'Front Up', *The Canberra Times*, 17 October 2005

The Highs and Lows of a Manic Life

I did a stand-up gig once – Raw Comedy, back in 2002. One thing that set me back was that I was manic when I did it. You know, very up.

Okay, a bit of Psychiatry 1005. I suffer from a condition that about one person in 100 has called bipolar disorder. The old name for this is manic depression.

People with bipolar suffer from sustained periods of mood swing, either up (mania) or down (depression).

Acute mania drives up the mood – with talkativeness, expansive or elated feelings, grandiose and disordered ideas or schemes, flights of fancy, sleeplessness, restless physical energy, strong appetites, irritability and egoism.

During mania a person is liable to bring ruin on their personal relationships, finances and job (if employed) in a spree which lasts for weeks, followed by a deep depression that often continues for months.

Only half the people with bipolar disorder work and one in five kill themselves. They also can have low level arrogance and irrationality.

To make matters worse, I also suffer from schizophrenia. When someone suffers from bipolar disorder and schizophrenia this is collectively known as schizoaffective disorder (bipolar type). This disorder affects about one in 200 people.

Having schizoaffective disorder (bipolar type), I suffer from positive and negative symptoms.

Positive symptoms refer to thoughts, perceptions and behaviours that are ordinarily absent in people in the general population, but are present in persons with schizoaffective disorder (bipolar type).

I experience hallucinations, thinking disturbances and delusions. The most common thing I have to deal with is delusions of reference. I often think that something in my environment is referring to me when actually it is not.

When this refers to people speaking, I call this a language only I can hear.

Negative symptoms are the absence of thoughts, perceptions or behaviours that are ordinarily present in people in the general population.

I suffer from blunted affect (diminished expressiveness of face, voice tone and gestures), apathy, anhedonia (deriving little or no pleasure from anything), poverty of speech and inattention.

Anyway, getting back to my stand-up set, I spoke for five minutes, got one laugh and thought I was going to win.

This is how you think when you're manic – it's like I'm going to win this, then I'm going on the Oprah Winfrey show, then I'm going to be a professional tennis player, then I'm going to be the Prime Minister of Australia.

I didn't win.

My current psychiatrist is cool. I once told him about a *Simpsons* episode whose writers made up an illness called geriatric profanity disorder. He leant back in his chair and said, 'Ah, GPD.'

Once, he was writing me a prescription. It fell off his desk, and he caught it on his shoe. He said, 'Still got it.'

My first psychiatrist was cool too.

I went in for a consultation wearing a T-shirt with the Beatles on it from their *Let It Be* days.

At the end, he asked me who the four men on my T-shirt were.

I said, 'The Beatles.'

He said, 'I never knew they looked like that.'

Michael Byrne is a 27-year-old unemployed man who spends his days looking for work, playing the bass and visiting the Florey bakery.

From 'Front Up', *The Canberra Times*, 27 March 2006

Pub poetry reading just like old days

The performance poetry scene in Canberra in the late 1990s was wild. You could turn up two or three nights a week to places and expect to read. There were readings at Tilley's, the Gypsy Bar, the Phoenix Bar, the Red Room and Heaven Nightclub. There were a number of regulars – Gerald Keaney, who had weird sideburns and a weirder box that, when stepped on, distorted his voice; Michael Dargaville, who had issues with almost everything; a cool public servant named Hal Judge; a tough nut named Anthony Hayes; those seductive temptresses Tarryn Ellis and Heather Catchpole and a younger version of myself.

The Phoenix Bar was my favourite place to read. I must admit I'm partial to a schooner of Guinness, which flowed freely at the Phoenix Bar. I could have a couple of schooners of Guinness, read, then stumble on to an Action bus that would take me to the Belconnen interchange. From there I would cruise home in a taxi. There were consequences from drinking Guinness, though. Once, I turned up to uni the next day with a hangover after drinking three schooners of Guinness.

Reading at the various nightclubs and bars was tough. The smoke got in your eyes and the punters could be apathetic and talkative. Once, at Heaven, a heckler called out something not very nice to me. I told him to kiss my assonance.

At the end of the millennium, the readings at the various nightclubs and bars stopped. The people organising lost interest and some of the regulars left Canberra.

Readings have started up at Toast and Section 57 but the scene these nights has lost the vibrancy that was there at the end of the last century. I went to the last reading at Heaven in 2000 and have been to relatively few since.

Although one night in 2002 at Toast some of the old magic was revived. It was a small, intimate, supportive crowd. There were candles on the tables. A magazine was being distributed. Everyone in the audience listened attentively. I put my name down to read. When it was my turn,

I walked to the microphone. As a tribute to the nightclub Toast, I decided to read my short ballad 'Toast' from my first book *Estuary at Dusk*. It got a lukewarm response. Not to be deterred, I decided next to go with my masterpiece 'Study of a Wrecked Car'. I introduced it as the best poem I had ever written. I've never been a reciter, but, after writing fifty drafts of the poem I found I knew it off by heart. I gave a flawless reading and it went down really well. The girls there were impressed.

It felt great, just like old times.

Michael Byrne is a 27-year-old poet. His second book, *Southbound*, is out now from Ginninderra Press.

From 'Panorama', *The Canberra Times*, 3 September 2011

Afloat on an Irish songline

Poetry
This Floating World By Libby Hart. Five Islands Press. 77pp. $21.95
Reviewer: Michael Byrne

This Floating World is Libby Hart's second collection of poetry. Her first, *Fresh News from the Arctic*, received the Anne Elder Award. Hart was born in 1971, and is one of about 30 younger-generation Australian female poets in this country at the moment. These young women are building a reputation for breaking conventional strictures in their poetry. They tend to be just as interested in the figurative as the literal and their work often delves into abstraction. These poets are, in a sense, going for more, and the reader has to make a leap of faith and 'believe' in what they are doing.

Fortunately, Hart's work is somewhat concrete. *This Floating World* is in two parts, the first being a suite of four poems with an undertone of intimacy that remains for the rest of the collection. Intimacy for Hart is, refreshingly, not overtly sexual and thus she achieves a certain dignity in the matter.

The second part contains a large number of monologues (collectively known as 'This floating world: a songline'), derived from a recent residency in Ireland. The reader is guided through the songline by an omnipotent force that listens to the monologues voiced not just by people but animals, places and things. The monologues also have a songlike quality to them. They are in free verse but achieve a certain verbal music through the eloquence of Hart's writing.

Apart from their musicality, the monologues have a dramatic aspect to them. *This Floating World* has been adapted for stage and performed in Australia. Most of the monologues have that necessary dramatic intensity to them. Some are vehicles for a delightfully offbeat sense of humour. There is variation in the voices and Hart gives her subjects empathy and dignity. She shows originality in giving personified landscapes a voice. Thus the reader gets (via a finished reading of *This Floating World*) a comprehensive sense of Ireland.

The titles in the collection act as a compass to point the reader in the right direction, instead of being merely decorative. What is crucial is the subject matter. The language used to describe it is very deliberate. For example, in 'Cow knee-deep in grass in a stone-walled field' an Irish cow will 'spend the hours/moving mouthful by mouthful'. The alliteration of the letter 'm' here deftly mimics the noise cows make eating.

The monologues are often short but not slight. All of them pass the long-established 'so what?' test. All have descriptive power, as in 'Northern fulmar nestled into stone' where 'wind and salted light weave in uptake/to power the push-and-drag beneath'. This is a superb description of the ocean, with its evocation of the fetch of the ocean working alongside the offshore wind. Fittingly, a separate line is given to each aspect of this.

This Floating World is more than rewarding; it is a collection of great generosity. As the monologues retain some considerable trace of the poet herself, Hart kindly offers something personal to the reader and should be commended for that. *This Floating World* is also generous in its exploration of Ireland – an Ireland that is described vividly and imaginatively. Hart's final and most important gift is her clarity. *This Floating World* is clear but not too clear. Even Hart's more abstract thoughts are not too much of a stretch.

Michael Byrne is a Canberra poet.

From 'Panorama', *The Canberra Times*, 19 November 2011

Poetic cool with wit and serious style

Poetry

Surface to Air By Jaya Savige. University of Queensland Press. 78pp. $24.95.

Reviewer: Michael Byrne

Surface to Air is Jaya Savige's second collection of poetry. His first, *Latecomers*, won the NSW Premier's Kenneth Slessor Prize and the Arts Queensland Thomas Shapcott Prize. Savige was born in 1978 and thus is one of the younger poets in the current Australian anthology *Thirty Australian Poets* (edited by Felicity Plunkett). In her particular sample, Plunkett brings together 30 younger-generation poets born in 1968 or later. She takes a number of poems from each poet. The poets in *Thirty Australian Poets*, as a whole, enjoy travel and are well educated. This can also be said of Savige – he proffers a number of poems set in Europe in *Surface to Air* and is currently studying for a PhD in English as a Gates Scholar at the University of Cambridge.

Surface to Air is divided into four parts: 'Snorkelling Lessons', 'Circular Breathing', 'A Brief History of Risk' and 'Memory Card'. This arrangement suggests an awareness of subject matter and consideration for the reader.

Savige shows consideration in other ways. He has just the right amount of clarity. He challenges the reader but he is not a difficult poet. He is undeniably clever, and parodies, the work of dead Australian poets (Michael Dransfield and John Forbes). He also cleverly uses wit, as in 'Pilot' where 'it's bouncers vs bikies, some gruff//mofo pulling a knife over a missing/shipment of meow meow'. This particular poem is very hip and cool. Not only that, it works well on the chosen language level. Savige uses modern vernacular to good effect.

There are other ways Savige writes well. He is technically subtle and sophisticated; he has a touch of the imagist (a necessity if a poet wants to create a sense of atmosphere) and he uses thought-provoking metaphors. An example can be found in 'Deciduous' where he describes children playing, while 'The sun is an old/grazed knee, weeping, unhealing'. The association between the sun and grazed knee is deft.

Surface to Air is full of memorable phrases. In the intense poem 'The Pain Switch', Savige comforts a woman in hospital. He grasps her hand and notes her 'vanquished sigh, a sharp, hot fist'. This is a brilliant last line. *Surface to Air* has a number of poems with last lines that harbour this sort of resolution. The fist stands as an appropriate and memorable symbol for a resolute woman.

The last poem in *Surface to Air* is the ambitious 'Riverfire'. It is about a gathering of people in a vibrant Brisbane (of which Savige is a part), where 'the city is alive, we comprise its thumping/pulse, its furore, coursing through intersections'. 'Riverfire' displays a kind of childish awe that the subject matter deserves. The reader shares his excitement. Again, there is a touch of the imagist in the way he describes his environs.

With Savige, we have a successful melding of the aesthetic (including his imagist nous) and the intellect; the two are not always in tandem in contemporary poetry. But in the poetry of Savige, they are both outstanding. One can also praise his tone quite easily – it is clinical, slick and clever. Savige is a mostly serious poet but uses wit to good effect. At this stage of his career he knows what he is doing. He never loses his poetic cool.

Michael Byrne is a Canberra poet.

From 'Panorama', *The Canberra Times*, 3 March 2012

A winning combination
Poetry
Edge Music By Stuart Cooke. Interactive Press. 82pp. $25.
Water Over Stone By Laura Jan Shore. Interactive Press. 78pp. $25.
Reviewer: Michael Byrne
Stuart Cooke's first full collection of poetry, *Edge Music*, is divided into three sections: the first, 'Corrosions', often finds Cooke overseas; the second 'Edge', often finds him with women; and 'Coast', the last sec-

tion, is quintessentially Australian in subject matter. Each section is about the same length and thus the collection is nicely balanced.

Cooke, who was born in 1980, last year completed a PhD in Indigenous Australian and Chilean poetics. He is interested in an eco-poetics, which allows energy to flow through language in the same way that flows constantly between different forms in an ecosystem. Correspondingly, he is most often a poet of exteriors, and the settings for his poems are more often than not various Australian areas.

Each poem is substantial. Some are shorter, but they are not slight. Cooke works solely in free verse, but achieves a wonderful variation in tone throughout the book. He also never misses a trick with titles.

Technically, Cooke is adept and achieves more variation through experimentation with enjambment. Take his habit of starting a word at the end of a line and finishing it at the start of the next. This may seem random and arbitrary, but it is certainly different.

There are differences in the level of clarity in *Edge Music*. Australian poet Robert Gray, in his imprimatur on the back cover, notes that *Edge Music* 'negotiates between opacity and lucidity'. It does this by way of not having extremes of both.

Everything used as material in *Edge Music* is handled by a healthy intellect. In 'Berlin World', after looking at a painting by Felix Schramm, Cooke notes, 'there is a global vacancy / – although global really / isn't the right / term: it's an individual / mourning / of a life lost or possibly never even / begun'.

The poetic analysis, evaluation and synthesis in this poem and others show a good capacity for higher-order thinking.

Cooke also chooses his subject matter well. As a traveller, he takes the reader to interesting places they have most likely never been before. Then Cooke often treats his subject matter very intelligently. A winning combination. With *Edge Music*, Cooke has invited the reader to engage with a book that is assured, unrushed and without a hint of pretension.

Laura Jan Shore's collection, *Water over Stone*, is also assured but for different reasons. Shore was born in 1950 in Manchester, England, and soon travelled to the United States with her American parents. In 1996, she emigrated to the Byron Shire, where she became involved with Dangerously Poetic, a community group seeking to encourage, publish and promote quality poetry from the Northern Rivers region of NSW. Some of Shore's poetry is set in this area, some in the US.

Shore is at her best when she is dealing with her family in the US. She writes with a seeming authenticity and a sense of fun. In 'Ungloved', an upper-class woman dismisses her gardener, takes off her gardening gloves and plunges her palm, 'into the damp, black soil'. Shore knows what to do with the last line here; she knows not to go for too much, and lets the action speak for itself.

Last lines are not the only aspect of her craft at which Shore excels. She also has a touch of the imagist (a necessity if a poet wants to create a sense of atmosphere). In 'Wilderness, untouched', she often lets her images do the talking, for example, 'A canopy quivering with foliage // snakes through our fantasies. / Hidden gullies, pockets of primeval ferns'. This poem proves to be lush and exotic, like others in the collection.

Water over Stone is also a collection with point and purpose. In 'Hospice', Shore makes some observations of an artist obsessed with the sky. Her final reflection is the most poignant. She writes, 'In the mirrored black tonight / lie a few pricks of light and the thin moon / of your pillowed cheek / wells upward'. Again, there is the low-key ending – she lets the observation speak for itself.

There are a number of other instances where Shore is equally clever. But unlike *Edge Music*, the most interesting aspect is not the intellect of the poet; rather, it is Shore's impressive aesthetic. *Water over Stone* proves to have clarity, a wide range of subject matter and variation of form. The poems contain humour, grace and beauty. All these aspects of Shore's aesthetic go a long way in the process of winning the reader over.

Michael Byrne is a Canberra poet.